Desert Governess

An Englishwoman's personal experience with the
Saudi Royal Family

Phyllis Ellis

Edited by Gordon Medcalf
Published by TravellersEye

Desert Governess

1st Edition

Published by TravellersEye Ltd

May 2000

Head Office:

60B High Street

Bridgnorth

Shropshire

WV16 4DX

United Kingdom

tel: (0044) 1746 766447

fax: (0044) 1746 766665

email: books@travellerseye.com

website: www.travellerseye.com

Set in Times

ISBN: 1903070015

Copyright 2000 Phyllis Ellis

For John with love

Contents

Acknowledgements

To the following authors, for permission to quote from their excellent books: Joanna Trollope (*Britannia's Daughters*); Kathy Cuddihy (*Saudi Customs and Etiquette*); Raqaiyyah Waris Maqsud (*Islam*); Haiffaa A Jawad (*The Rights of Women in Islam*); Ruth Roded (*Women in Islam and the Middle East*). To Messrs Rogers & Hammerstein for permission to quote a lyric from *The King and I*.

My loving appreciation goes to my elder son Richard, a computer wizard who over the months has patiently guided me in times of acute frustration and confusion, as I slowly learned the necessary technical skills to prepare my book.

I also acknowledge with love and gratitude my younger son Jason, who helped me to give structural form to my copious notes and set me thinking about chapter headings and a title. His encouragement and support in the initial stages got me off the ground!

Last but not least to my publisher Dan Hiscocks who took notice of my manuscript, to my editor Gordon Medcalf and to all at TravellersEye especially Jill Ibberson, with warm thanks for their hard work and their enduring faith in me.

Characters

<u>Saudi Royal Family</u>

H.R.H.Prince Muqrin bin Abdul Aziz Al-Saud	Brother of King Fahd of Saudi Arabia.
Princess Abtah	Mother of the royal children.
Prince Faisal	Eldest son - lives and works in Jeddah.
Princess Hannah	Married to Prince Faisal - grand daughter of the late King Khalid.
Princess Lamia	Eldest daughter - lives in Riyadh.
Prince Abdul Aziz	Lamia's husband - high ranking army and police official.
Prince Bander	Aged 17 - royal student.
Princess Jowaher	Aged 14 - royal student
Princess Sarah	Aged 9 - royal student.

Associates of the Royal Family

Mr Hanif   Royal representative in London

Gabby   American wife of former
                         manager of Prince Muqrin's farm
                         - a good friend of Princess Abtah

Royal Cousins and Jowaher's Friends

Shoroq   Aged 16 and Hela aged 18,
                         sisters, and cousins of Jowaher -
                         living in Riyadh

Shou-Shou   Jowaher's best friend aged 16,
                         grandaughter of Muma Hasna.

Hoda   Friend of Jowaher, aged 17,
                         living in Hail

Ladies of the Palace

Soha   Wife of the Palace Manager.

Maha   Wife of a Palace driver.

Muma Hasna   Princess Abtah's Nanny when
                         she was a child - now aged 80.

Palace Staff

Charles   Prince Muqrin's personal aide - from India.

Hanan   Private tutor for Arabic - from Syria.

Rita   Sarah's Nanny - from the Philippines.

Lynda   Jowaher's Nanny - from the Philippines.

Muma Fozia   Cook - from Egypt.

Zahara   Princess Abtah's personal servant - from Ethiopia.

Rahma   Coffee bearer - from Eritrea.

Nefisa   Incense bearer - from Eritrea.

Rose   Palace seamstress - from the Philippines.

Palace Drivers

Ahmed   From Pakistan.

Nasr   From Sudan.

Ladies of Hail

Faiza   Socialite friend of Princess
                        Abtah.

Bedour   Doctor and visitor to the Palace
                        – from Syria.

Howazeen   Saudi teacher at the Ladies'
                        College.

Hala   Teacher of English at Jowaher's
                        school - from Egypt.

Saudi Arabia is a very private country, the Saudi Royal Family even more so. This book has not been written to pry into or abuse that privacy. It has been written in the hope of a better understanding of the country, culture, Muslim beliefs and ways of the people.

The insight into Saudi Royal life has been written with the greatest of respect. I would like to thank the Royal Family for the privilege of the adventure.

Introduction

This book tells how I, the writer, a middle-aged widow, an actor, singer and dancer, a teacher of English as a Foreign Language and also of Yoga, was engaged, in the best *The King and I* tradition, as a Governess by part of the Saudi Arabian Royal Family. It goes on to tell how I became immersed in the Arab lifestyle, with no expatriate company of any sort, and how I carried out my task in the complete absence of guidelines, living in a heavily guarded marble Palace in the Saudi Arabian desert.

After describing the initial shock of my encounter with an alien society, I share my personal journey of discovery as I went through a cultural, social and religious re-education, in a sustained effort to adapt and integrate successfully.

The book evolved out of curiosity and respect. Interwoven into the story is my insight into modern - and privileged - Saudi life.

Primarily my own story, the book also explores my impressions of Islam and the *Qur'an*; Muslim beliefs, customs, traditions and morality; hospitality and leisure; Saudi and Bedouin cuisine, dress, the family, modern women, marriage and divorce.

To go back (literally) to the very beginning, I am an Essex girl, born in 1939, the only child of Elsie and Jack Ellis. I will always be deeply grateful to my mother, who was determined to give me the advantages and opportunities that her parents were not able to give her. From an early age I attended ballet, drama and music lessons. My first stage appearance was at the age of five in a dancing school show at the Ilford town hall. Many more shows followed, plus the hard work and discipline of the Royal Academy of Dancing ballet, drama and music exams.

My mother applied for an Essex County Major Award for me to attend the Arts Educational School in London. The thought of going to an exciting school in a wonderful place like London really fired my imagination. Even in my youth I had a sense of adventure, preferring adventure stories and books about distant places.

The six years I spent at the school gave a new dimension to my life. The dance teachers were especially wonderful; for ballet we sometimes had stars like Alicia Markova and others from the Festival Ballet, and for contemporary dance we all worshipped Gillian Lyne, choreographer of the musical *Cats* and an ex-pupil. Her new ideas, style of dance and choreography were revolutionary at that time in the fifties.

The majority of the pupils were girls. One boy we girls had a passion for was David Hemmings, a star of the sixties. Most of us dreamed of going on the stage, and many achieved their ambitions in my time: Francesca Annis, Valerie Singleton, Toots Lockwood and Dennis Waterman.

I am sure we all longed for stardom, but it was exciting just to be working. I signed my first contract aged eighteen years and seven months. I had a new name to go with my new career: "Tricia Ellis . . .yes, it's got more of a 'showbiz' ring about it!" the impresario Rex Newman insisted. So I made my debut in the *Fol-de-Rols* at the White Rock Pavilion in Hastings - the show was quite famous: Arthur Askey and Kenneth Horne once topped the bill! I was engaged as a 'soubrette', who sings, dances and acts in comedy sketches. I began to be typecast as a comedienne and appeared in TV shows with comedians Benny Hill, Ted Ray, Leslie Crowther, Morecambe & Wise, and Harry Worth in the play *Scoop,* an adaptation of Evelyn Waugh`s novel.

I was lucky to work in repertory companies, and in the seventies took part in the highbrow and at that time sensational erotica *Oh, Calcutta!* devised by Kenneth Tynan, with sketches by Samuel Beckett and John Lennon, at the Royalty theatre in London. My family also tease me about my claim to fame as a mum in TV commercials for Fairy Liquid, Persil and 'don't forget the fruit gums, Mum,' the latter directed by Tony Scott!

During the inevitable periods of 'resting' between jobs I discovered The Open University, which gives married women like myself, with a family to look after and possibly a part or full-time job, opportunities for further education and a whole new lease of life.

I would never have started a degree course, never mind finished one, had my late husband John not seen my need, suggested the solution, and unfailingly encouraged me when the role of mature student, on top of all my professional and family roles, seemed to have beaten me. John opened a door for me, ushered me through, and supported me until I could walk alone. Words cannot express my deepest love and thanks.

With a degree, and drama and dance qualifications, I could widen my job search. Part-time tutor for the performing arts course at my local college in Southend taught me a great deal, especially an unforgettable project I initiated, set up and ran to enable mentally-handicapped students to join with the other students for drama improvisation sessions.

With my Teaching English as a Foreign Language (TEFL) qualifications I travelled to places I couldn't otherwise have afforded to visit and I had nerve-wracking and wonderful times. Briefly in Italy, I set up, ran and acted in an English Language Theatre Company. We presented my adaptations of Shakespeare's *A Midsummer Night's Dream,* Bernard Shaw's *Pygmalion* and Harold Pinter's *Night Out.* I formed the company with professional Italian and English actors, and we performed in arts and community centres.

And so, eventually, my footsteps led me to Saudi Arabia, a great experience. This book evolved partly as a record, and partly from my wish to encourage others to launch out and surprise themselves as I have done, and most importantly in the hope of promoting in a small way a better understanding of a fascinating country and culture.

Princess Sarah aged nine, the youngest child of my employers, HRH Prince Muqrin bin Abdul Asiz al Saud and his wife Princess Abtah often said to me, with a curiously wicked smile on her face:

"Phyllis - what you think - of my country, my Palace - my family?"

I always passed the question off with: "Oh, one day I'll tell you, Sarah." Princess Sarah, your reading skills, when I left the Palace, had improved enormously. Please read this book and you will learn the answer to your question!

Chapter One

A Spirit of Adventure

The advertisement reads: *'English Governess for Prince and Princesses of Saudi Royal Family.'* Governess? The title intrigues me, conjuring up images of a Victorian era, when a position as governess was desperately sought by many an educated woman on her own without other means of support.

Do I also have to become a governess?

I am recently widowed, left only with my husband's debts and I need to find a new start in life. Searching for courage, I hurry to my bookshelves to try to remember what I have read in the past about governesses. Shirley, in Charlotte Bronte's novel of the same name, held the position in low esteem: 'Be a governess? Better be a slave at once.' Joanna Trollope writes in *Britannia's Daughters*: 'They were outcasts from life both below and above stairs.'

Reading more, my own opinion grows that tribute should be

paid to the tenacity and enterprise of these women in socially repressed times. From humble beginnings in Britain, by the end of the nineteenth century: 'the status of the governess abroad was to be envied.' (Joanna Trollope). This is exemplified by the legendary Anna Leonowens, who, in 1862 accepted King Mongkut of Siam's offer to instruct twenty-five princes and princesses of the royal blood, later inspiring the musical and Hollywood movie *The King and I*.

I always wanted to travel, but lack of money was a problem until my sons grew able to look after themselves. Then I took an extra qualification to teach English as a foreign language. Eight years teaching in Italy, Greece and Spain has shown me how to meet each foreign country on its own terms, how to assimilate a new culture, how to accept some enormous differences.

Seeing the Middle East has been an ambition for a long time. The enigma of Arab culture fascinates me, even though my friends and family are sceptical: 'Saudi Arabia? Oh, I wouldn't go there' - 'Dicey, very dicey' - 'What about white slave traffic?' - 'Will we ever see you again?'

"It's a rich country" I retort, "and I need the money." Suddenly I want to know more about this quintessentially English occupation and a spirit of adventure takes hold, so I apply for the job.

"Can you come for an interview at 11.30am?" Mr Hanif, a representative of the Saudi Royal Family has responded to my CV, telephoning to invite me for an interview at the Royal Family's London house. I put the phone down.

Should I go? Is this an opportunity not to miss? Have I the strength to travel into the unknown? How do I make a decision like this without John? I was married for thirty years and whatever I did, I talked over with John. Tears of grief and loss start, as they do each morning when I wake up alone. I am not sure, not for one minute, not until the day of the interview arrives.

Feeling nervous, I am early and walk about in nearby St. James's Park, practising Yogic breathing to calm me down. With five minutes to spare, I ring the intercom. The door is opened by a sophisticated, young woman.

"Hello, do come in, you must be Phyllis. I'm Suzanne, Mr Hanif's daughter." Suzanne is a practising lawyer in London. Their family is Palestinian.

I learn that the royal governess is expected to be strict with the three children aged seventeen, fourteen and nine. Her English lessons are in the afternoon, after the children return from their Arabic schools and have their siestas. She accompanies the children to those schools and back in a limousine and she may never sit in the front seat of a royal car, take a taxi or drive a car. Alcohol is forbidden in Saudi Arabia, and videos or photographs of anyone showing bare flesh, even arms or legs. The English governess must keep her own head and arms covered outside the royal palace, and she is not ever permitted to be alone with a man.

I leave with mixed feelings. The salary is much lower than I was expecting. I feel afraid…of who, and what, is waiting for me in the desert in Saudi Arabia.

Mr Hanif has accepted my refusal to sign a written contract. With a verbal contract I can simply leave. Is that so? Or is the royal governess a prisoner inside a royal palace?

What if I can't get out? Once there I can't go to a travel agent and buy a ticket home. Mr Hanif said I would need a visa to leave, and that would have to be signed - by one of the Royal Family.

In the past, if I had been in trouble, anywhere in the world, John would always have found me, and rescued me. He was my knight in shining armour, and now I cannot call on John any more.

The phone rings the next day:

"Phyllis, this is Mr Hanif. Can you be ready to leave for Saudi Arabia in ten days?"

I have got the job! But I cannot raise the salary, however hard I try.

I say I will ring him back. I give myself one more day to think about it.

I *would* be getting free accommodation and meals…I *could* save money…what would I spend it on, in a remote desert, where public entertainment is forbidden?

It is no good asking my sons and friends again…I have to make my own decision…I have to… Impulsively, I ring his number and accept the post.

"I expect the weather will be very hot when I arrive." I say to Mr Hanif.

"No," he answers, "just wear what you are wearing now in England."

An astonishing response. In my head are pictures of burning desert, camels, dates, palm trees, goats, sheep, bells, dusty roads, brightly coloured carpets, big camp fires, a coffee pot steaming, a circle of seated figures under the stars, black tents…the sexual appetite of Arab men.

"It is late December…you may get frost…the temperature can be five or ten degrees below zero."

I rush to my atlas and encyclopaedia. Where am I going? In a vast expanse of desert, up near the Iraqi border in the remote north

26

of the country is a tiny dot called Hail. My God…I am going *there*…I am terrified. I hug the atlas to myself and find I am weeping, but my courage returns and into my suitcase go vests, gloves, a woolly hat, and, hoping as always for good luck, a bikini.

"Are there any English school books?" I ask Mr Hanif.

"I don't know…maybe the other teachers leave books behind…you can buy some…I will repay all books money."

So I have no briefing. Except I will be teaching a prince aged seventeen, and two princesses aged fourteen and nine. Creating and preparing suitable material when I arrive wouldn't pose a problem, but all the rest would have to be guess work.

I buy Intermediate level English course books and listening tapes for the two eldest children. Also a Robyn Davidson adventure story adapted for young foreign speakers of English, about crossing the Australian desert alone with two camels. That should give a fourteen year old girl in a closed society an idea of freedom. What will a seventeen year old prince brought up in Arabian grandeur identify with? I go for abridged flying adventures and Jean-Jacques Cousteau diving stories.

For the nine year old, an adapted version of *Black Beauty*, English children's songs: *The wheels on the bus go round and round…, If you're happy and you know it clap your hands…,* and brightly illustrated Read and Listen teaching aids.

For myself, Jane Austen, Wordsworth, George Eliot, an essential *Get by in Arabic* dictionary and a pile of music tapes. Noel Coward singing *Mad Dogs and Englishmen* and *The Stately Homes of England* which are hilarious and help me get through times of homesickness.

In go my First Aid box, TCP, garlic pearls and Olbas Oil for colds. Primrose Oil and Aloe Vera face cream, mascara, eye-shadow, ear plugs. Cotton wool, needles, scissors, safety-pins and, as I am an English lady, a flannel and a back scrubber. Mr Hanif advises an umbrella. I don't dare take a corkscrew, or my huge farewell box of liqueur chocolates.

Saudi Arabian Customs make rigorous searches I am told. Any magazines with pictures of naked women are confiscated and you're in trouble. I am scared packing. I do re-label my video of Zefferelli's *Romeo and Juliet* film and name it 'English Country Gardens'!

Mr Hanif hands me my ticket at the check-in desk. "Good luck…remember me to the Royal Family…you will be met at the airport…if you are not happy…telephone me…goodbye."

The plane journey is unbelievable. One by one each man disappears into the toilet. He goes in wearing a suit and tie. He emerges wearing a long white off-the-shoulder number - one bare shoulder is a Muslim symbol of male bodily strength.

They lay prayer mats down anywhere in the aircraft, the aisles, by the toilets, in the kitchen area. Every man has his mat and kneels on it bowing. The white-robed bottoms lift up beside our seats. Big fat men praying send our food trays flying…I almost lose hold of mine.

"They're on a pilgrimage to Makkah…*Ramadan*…you know," whispers the stewardess clearing up a mess.

A driver meets me at the airport. "Me Ahmed – Pakistan. You – fly America?"

"No, I'm Phyllis – English – I flew from London Heathrow."

"You English – good. No like – this American – Clinton – bad man – Hilary Clinton good woman – she wear the pants – Clinton no keep pants on."

Ahmed is turning out to be quite a character.

I have flown an hour on from Jeddah. Now we drive from the airport on a tarmac road into desert scrub.

As the sun sets silhouetting a mountain range, the sky turns fiery red and I start to hear the sounds of calling in the air. Ahmed says "*Allah akbar, Allah akbar*…God is great Phyllis…God is great."

He reaches into a plastic bag by his seat and stuffs dates into his mouth and swills back water from a bottle. In the back of the car I see his hand offering dates to me. I don't want to be impolite so I take them. The fresh taste is succulent and delicious. It is a wonderful moment.

Ahmed is wiping his mouth with the end of his *ghutra* – his red and white check head covering. He breaks his fast at sunset with dates and water because it is *Ramadan*. Now I understand.

These compelling calls to prayer ring out from the hundred mosques of Hail. As dusk falls the car turns at a board sign for 'Aja Palace' and in the distance along the dusty track the lights of Hail appear. High fortress walls guide our way to an iron entrance gate.

Armed security guards in khaki uniform with guns wave us through. All the security guards wear bomber jackets and green berets, trousers are tucked into jack-boots, and many of them have thick black moustaches or black beards.

I arrive at the Grand Marble Palace of HRH Prince Muqrin bin Abdul Azis al Saud, brother of the King…my new home.

Ahmed drives though an iron gate past an oyster marble building high as a five storey house and wide as three English town houses – the Administration Centre.

The Palace is entered by two bronze doors that remind me of the great Baptistry doors in Florence.

Ahmed draws up to the Princess's door. I will never enter the Palace by the Prince's door. Men and women live apart.

I step out of the back of the car onto pale pink and cream and beige paving. Ahmed pushes the Princess's door open. I see an enormous oyster marble staircase with wrought iron banisters and I think of Cinderella.

Ahmed says, "Come. The Princess is in her sitting-room." He walks up the staircase beside me. At the top he leaves me in front of gold-edged white double-doors open for me to see Princess Abtah on her big sofa watching TV.

At the top all the doors are closed except one through which I [...] long cheap-looking table with a plastic tablecloth designed [...] little tiny red, green and blue flowers. A dozen cream coloured [...]-back painted wooden chairs are round the table. On the cream [...] are two wooden cream wall cupboards. There is a stand-up [...]ooker and an enormous fridge filled with milk and vegetables. [...]e found the Princess's kitchen where the women's daily meals [...] aten.

Oh for good quality tea leaves and a china teapot. I find an [...]ic kettle and teabags. Flat unleavened bread and *hummus* fill [...]p. This is my first lesson in fending for myself which turns out [...] the key to my life in this Palace.

[...]e afternoon I sit on the back seat of a Cadillac. I am shrouded [...]ack. I have boldly asked Princess Abtah if I may go out of the [...]e grounds to shop for my own kitchen. Soon after I hear a [...]k on my bedroom door.

"Princess say wear this."

Zahara, a small African woman from Eritrea, comes in. [...]tly she ties my *burqa* at the back of my head. The *burqa* is a [...]mask made from soft black material with openings for my eyes. [...]nic law forbids women to show their faces in public.

Next she stands behind me, still silently, holding out a black [...]n. An *abaya* is a floor-length cloak with sleeves. Last comes [...]arha, a black gauze scarf to cover my head.

[...]e car I hate the mask. The air conditioning is on but I cannot

Chapter Two

The First Day

Sounds of wailing wake me and at first I don't recognise what I am hearing. I am very tired. Exhausted. Then I remember what Ahmed told me about the call to prayer.

My bed is a four poster as big as three single beds. I lie gazing up at the canopy of silk patterned with green and pale pink flowers. The four curtains are tied back with cream braid and all the walls of my large room are covered with matching floral silk. Panels of mirrors and French windows under a moulded plaster ceiling create an airy, spacious feel I shall enjoy.

The floor is cream marble with a sky blue thick carpet. I forgot how high off the ground my bed was when I clambered up into it the night before and I fell on the carpet twisting my ankle. My limp lasts for three days.

When I pull back the curtains as far as I can see are the lovely pale pink, green and blue paved paths between date trees and palms. Fig trees and pomegranates surround a circular cream marble fountain. In the dark I did not realise my view is across the gardens. My apartment is on the ground floor and seeing a gardener at work outside, I feel anxious at how vulnerable my rooms are to enter. I shall keep the tall windows locked night and day.

The bathroom has mirrors on the ceiling and all the walls…I am truly embarrassed…wherever I look I can see myself!

I lie in the wonderful bed and remember my arrival. I could hardly believe the warm-hearted welcome I was given. There was no standing on ceremony. We spoke in English. The Princess was insistent that I called home to tell my sons I had arrived safely and a servant brought me a telephone.

I met Prince Bander who is seventeen, Princess Jowaher who is fourteen and Princess Sarah who is nine. Prince Muqrin is away hunting and I had the sense not to say to the Princess that I would like to see falconry – a traditional desert sport in Saudi Arabia. It is an awful breach of etiquette for a woman to ask a wife about her husband…she might be interested in him!

My rooms are in the Study Building a short walk from the Palace. All my luggage was taken there and left outside the door. I hardly took in what was happening except that supper was at midnight, which is traditional in *Ramadan*. Another meal is often served before sunrise.

I confessed to my tiredness and said I was not accustomed to eating through the night, and I walked carefully down the long sweeping staircase, through the huge bronze Princess's Door and out into the chill early morning air. On the way to my rooms I felt profound relief. I had made it so far.

This morning I feel terribly guilty that I am g
I limp out into the beautiful garden. The sun is brig
of sunglasses and sun cream on my face and whi
early January breeze sends me back in to find a ca
the far north of Saudi Arabia.

I walk alone up and down paths where leme
grapefruit shine in the trees. It is the citrus fruit se
was coming to a desert and I find an oasis on my
soul is about and I grow a little scared. Standing
the heady perfume of white jasmine and suddenly a
makes me jump.

"Mornin', Ma'am." A Filipino workman is
underground irrigation system. Jets of water beg
glistening in the sunlight.

"Where is Princess Abtah?" I ask him.

"No one wake up, Ma'am. Maybe two or aft
day night – night day."

"When do we eat?"

"Eat six o'clock Ma'am."

I am hungry. Actually I am shattered. Wha
Fasting from sunrise to sunset and disoriented by
am overwhelmed with the strangeness of it all, and
pull my cardigan tight around my body and reali
governess solitude and loneliness did not end with th

I need a nice cup of tea.

The kitchen in my rooms is utterly empty. I
paving and push open the Princess's door into the P
up the pale tall marble staircase. I must go up this
again all alone.

breathe. I open the window and think I am going to faint. The mask is hot and claustrophobic and maddening...but I want to keep my job. Hail is a conservative stronghold of Bedouin traditions and Islamic principles. I must conform. I must respect this oh so foreign culture. The Cadillac glides past herds of sheep and goats grazing in the scrub. My identity has disappeared. I am anonymous.

And I could be punished. The *muttawa* are the moral and religious guardians easily spotted with their long beards and chastising sticks. They parade the *souks* usually beside a policeman, checking each woman has her face covered, and is wearing a skirt to her feet. I see two young men who are trying to flirt with some young women and talk to them in the street being fiercely reprimanded by the *muttawa*.

This visit to a supermarket is a real adventure outside the Palace walls. A Palace employee cannot just walk out. I have to get permission from Princess Abtah. The Princess has to ring and ask if a driver is free. Women may not use taxis in Hail and the law forbids females to drive a vehicle.

I am the only single woman in the supermarket. In Hail women shop only with their husband or their family. My driver waits at the checkout and I am conspicuous. My face itches inside the *burqa*. I bravely pull it off. I need to put on my glasses to see what is on the shelves. Now I am attracting attention. Solitary men stare hard at me. I am anxious and cross and remember English warnings about the sexual appetite of Arab men particularly towards blue-eyed blondes.

I want protection. Perhaps I do need my *burqa*.

In this country a woman's place is in the home. No theatres or cinemas or concert halls or discos or clubs or places of public entertainment for her, by law. All alcohol is forbidden.

I am to be the only English woman in Hail, and I will live only with women. The sexes are segregated. We – the women – meet and socialise inside houses. It is against the law for a woman to be alone with a man who is not her husband or a close relative. Adultery is horribly punished by families and by law.

Neither I nor the princesses nor any woman may travel alone. If we go out with a woman friend or relative we must take with us written permission from a husband or a close relative. It looks like I shall need some luck and courage to go anywhere.

And who will I talk to I wonder? It is true that English is the working language in the Palace because English is how the migrant workers communicate. They come from the Philippines, Bangladesh, Pakistan, India, Sudan and Ethiopia, and I have discovered the office staff are fluent. Drivers and servants, who I suspect I shall spend my time with, can hardly converse at all. I don't mind speaking slowly and clearly or miming and throwing myself about as if I am playing charades. I have done that teaching in Greece, Spain and Italy. But shall I have any intimate friends?

So far I sense utter strangeness. Faceless women in black move and talk together as if they are choreographed…a kind of tribal unity from which I shall be excluded.

In Hail the burning *oude* wood perfumes the air along with spices from cooking pots. Arabic music from radios, and waves of prayer chants and wails from the mosques mesmerise and enthral me. I long to wander about and discover this strange new world I am in but I am taken straight back to the royal car.

The Palace building is all oyster marble walls outside and inside. Banqueting and reception rooms are hung with silk fabrics in gorgeous pastel colours between gold mirrored panels and windows as tall as two floors of my English home. Heavy dark blinds block out the sun.

It is a challenge to find enough confidence to follow the labyrinth of corridors and rooms. Many doors are kept locked for security and a guard has to be called by telephone to bring the key. I hear their steps far off on the marble floors and then silence as they cross the rich deeply patterned carpets underneath intricate glass chandeliers. Security cameras watch me inside the Palace and all over the garden. I do not know if I am watched in my own rooms.

Huge life-size colour photographs of the Royal Family hang on the Palace walls as if they are film stars.

In the royal residence the colours are formal. Pleasing cool beige, cream, shades of brown and fresh apple green. Large comfy sofas and huge armchairs are scattered around the television. Thick pale velvet backs the upright occasional chairs.

Royal and guest apartments stand separately in the Palace grounds and I am amazed by the spaciousness. Bedrooms, bathrooms, receptions rooms, sitting rooms, a kitchen in every one.

I discover a swimming pool in our quarters. Apparently there is another pool in the men's quarters too. Swimming will be my physical recreation I guess. I shall not be out on the football pitch and there are no other sports or games. Oh well, I tell myself. Mustn't grumble. It's not every day an Englishwoman gets to live in an Arabian Palace. Make the most of it Phyllis!

A bouquet of flowers is lying on my study desk. A surprise as there are no cut flowers anywhere. I ask a servant who says the flowers were presented to Princess Abtah at a community event and she has given them to me. I did talk to her about flowers and I am touched she has remembered. Holding them I miss John and the boys. My tears start up again.

I have no lessons to teach until after *Eid-al-fitre.*

"When's that?" I ask Princess Jowaher.

"We don't know yet. Look for the new moon. That will be the first day."

I look at her flabbergasted, not understanding at all.

"We count by the moon. Not the sun."

In my room I check the facts. The *Hijira* calendar started in 622AD when the prophet Muhammed and his followers left Makkah for Madinah to escape persecution. So the year 1997 AD corresponds to 1417/1418 here. And the *Hijira* year is eleven days shorter than our Gregorian year. Now I am even more confused…and this is only the beginning.

Saudis also follow a solar astrological calendar that corresponds to the Gregorian calendar except that the months are called by Zodiac names. School holidays and the national budget go by the Zodiac calendar.

Ramadan is the ninth month of the Muslim year celebrating God's first revelations to the Prophet Muhammed which went on for twenty-three years. *Ramadan* month is for spiritual growth. Every day between dawn and dusk Muslims keep away from food and drink, and sensual pleasures. Surely this makes the nights even more romantic?

I wish I was not alone and in the evening, to calm the fantasies in my exhausted mind, I go out into the serenity of the gardens. A magical twilight blue sky is full of stars. Sorrow and tension leave me as I walk the paved paths under the darkening fruit. I look up and a sliver of crystal clear new moon hangs alongside a radiant star that I feel I can touch . I shall teach the royal children tomorrow.

Chapter Three
Princess Abtah's Sitting Rooms

Sitting for long periods of time is an art. The Saudi Royal Family circle has it. In the mornings they sit in Princess Abtah's day sitting-room from ten until lunch is served in the kitchen-diner next door, and then they sit again till three in the afternoon, siesta time. An enormous television dominates the room. The ladies watch programmes from Lebanon – the Hollywood channel which shows sex and violence is banned by Princess Abtah.

The royal day sitting-room door is always open unless Princess Abtah is away or asleep. Her sofa is at the head of the circle of chairs and sofas for the women and she warmly welcomes everyone. Easy royal access still exists as a legacy from the Bedouin leader in his tent where anyone could come with problems or to gossip, to recite poetry or just to sit and drink coffee.

From my first day Princess Abtah, whose formal title is *Amira*, often telephones me with a good morning greeting and an invitation to take coffee. Her manner is in no way superior, she speaks in a low, sexy voice, giving orders simply and directly. I never hear her raise her voice, though she doesn't stand any nonsense. Nothing escapes her notice – I think the drivers and servants are directed to bring her news of anything going on inside the Palace and the locality.

Daughter of a tribal chief of Hail, Princess Abtah is still naturally beautiful in middle age. Though she's a granny, her comely, rounded figure always looks good in her colourful embroidered kaftans or her long skirts and tailored jacket suits, or her gorgeous designer dresses. She seems to be loved and respected by all, and armed with a personal mobile and the internal phones, she supervises the constant royal banquets, parties and outings – a Mother Earth figure.

Muma Hasna, Princess Abtah's old nanny, is in the day sitting-room every morning, often with Princess Lamia and Princess Hannah. Relatives come and go, drivers from the airport carry in packages full of the latest European kitchen gadgets, hand-made chocolates, and for a while a daily hamper is delivered from a Health Clinic in Riyadh full of organic food for Princess Sarah to help her lose weight – Sarah calls it her 'Phyllis food' and shares it with me, which is lovely of her.

Shoes are left outside the door. Servants enter for orders. Hanan, the children's Arab Studies tutor, comes in to sit and answers Princess Abtah's questions about how the children are doing and sometimes Hanan reads the ladies' fortunes in coffee grains in the bottom of cups.

After school the children always go straight in to see their mother and fling themselves at her with hugs and kisses and put their heads on her shoulder, while she cuddles them and hears all the school news.

A lesson can be learned here in patience and repose but I get fidgety and bored after about an hour's sitting. I can't understand the gossip though Princess Abtah does her best to speak English and to include me in conversations. So I make an excuse that I have to work and go to my rooms.

Occasionally I can arrange to go shopping. It's quite a business. First I telephone Princess Abtah and she says, 'I don't know Phyllis – maybe no driver – wait'. So I wait. If she calls she says, 'Phyllis – you come', and I have to run out right away. In the car is my obligatory chaperone – it is usually someone who speaks a little English, one of the teenage daughters of the Palace staff or Gabby, *Amira's* American friend.

I do buy some gold earrings in the *souk* in Hail. Ahmed stands watching. I realise now that he is expected to spy on me at all times I am out, and to tell Princess Abtah where I've been and what I've said and done. Gabby takes me to one of the little horseshoe-shaped stalls and tells me the prices. The gold is weighed. I try to bargain. Gabby discovers from the shop assistant that the stall owner is the Palace telephone operator so I should attempt to bargain with him. He is always asleep, eating or praying and for days I try to reach him. Gabby makes a deal with the stall holder for me and eventually I go back and get my earrings. Jewellery traditionally indicates status in Arabic culture, but for me the earrings may be a useful source of cash in hard times.

Saudi society is intensely private. To protect and preserve its traditions the country is not freely open to strangers, entry and exit visas must be supplied by a sponsor. No tourist visas are issued, mail is censored and women travelling alone are regarded with suspicion.

Fortunately for me when I arrived at the airport my VIP status meant I had an airport hostess to guide me through the thorough and chaotic customs baggage search. I remember the sound of her voice and gentle manner but I wished I could see what she looked like behind her black face mask.

In the afternoons when Prince Muqrin comes home from his work Princess Abtah disappears with him to bed for the siesta time. About five they get up, have coffee, and she starts to get dressed and ready for the daily reception in the *diwaniyah* - evening sitting-room.

The first time I attend this ritual session I wear my fitted, sleeveless calf-length dress and discover it is impolite to show armpits – only a few of my dresses will be acceptable here. I also learn that the male cleaners complain to Princess Abtah if I leave underclothes drying in my bathroom or anywhere within their sight – apparently the last governess was fired for that and for smoking cigarettes in her rooms. I am learning that nowhere is really private.

The evening sitting-room is formal and gigantic. Princess Abtah still sits on her sofa but in the evenings she sits alone, down at the far end of a long brightly-coloured carpet. In we come one by one, walk down the carpet towards her and exchange kisses, first with Princess Abtah and then with all the ladies present, sometimes fifty. Royal ladies kiss noses as well as cheeks – the nose is considered a noble feature.

It is a special party of *Eid* and I manage to say the Arab salutation *'salaam alaikum'* – peace be with you, and the reply *'wa alaikum as salaam'* – and upon you peace. My pronunciation efforts make the ladies laugh and smile with congratulation.

The usual ritual to welcome guests is with coffee served in the evenings by two young girls from Eritrea – Rahma and Nafisa. In their pale purple and bright pink patterned shifts and flowing headscarves they drift serenely around and their fresh, youthful dark beauty fascinates me.

The brass Arab coffee pot – *dallah* – has a long beak spout and coffee is served in egg-cup small white china cups with geometric patterns. Mint tea always follows in small handled glasses, which I enjoy – Arabian coffee has cardamom added which takes a lot of getting used to.

To welcome royal guests an incense burner – *medkhana* – is brought in and taken round to each guest, who takes it and waves the aromatic smoke into her hair, shushing it over her body, and then she lifts her long skirt at the front and swings the burner under it – a legacy from Bedouin tribal times when there were no baths I guess! Incense smoke starts my eyes streaming and sends me into a sneezing fit – from now on I shall make a quick exit to the toilet when the *medkhana* appears!

The wealthy ladies who come to visit the Princess each have two or three servants and time to beautify themselves. Henna is used to enhance the hair, hands and feet, and *kohl* beautifies the eyes. With the ancient art of *mehndi* – of Egyptian and Indian origin – henna creates temporary intricate designs on the hands and feet of women for special occasions. It is mixed with eucalyptus oil and lemon juice to make a paste and a bag like a cake-icing container squeezes patterns onto the skin. For everyday use the mixture is spread onto the soles of the feet, toenails, palms and fingertips. It takes some time to dry and set. Ancient Arab belief was that the henna mixture kept the skin cool in the intense sunlight.

Kohl, a shiny black substance, is painted onto the eyelid and around the eye margin to give a dark, mystical, exotic look. Bedouin women believed it shielded their eyes from the glare of the sun's rays.

Abayas are left at the door and evening dress is varied. A popular outfit is a long, straight skirt with a slit at the back, worn with a long-sleeved, hip-length, tailored matching jacket. The middle-aged and older ladies prefer this style of dress or a kaftan. Trousers with a long tunic or blouse are also popular. Fashionable women wear designer label dresses or clothes made for them by their personal dressmaker. Hair is parted in the middle, drawn back into a bun at the nape of the neck and covered with a small gauze or chiffon scarf wound round over a black hairnet. More up-to-date styles are apparently available from hairdressers in Riyadh and Jeddah.

Dinner is served around ten o'clock. I arrive about half an hour before to avoid the 'gossiping hours'. When my eyes used to glaze over with boredom I often asked Princess Lamia, *Amira's* married daughter who lived in Riyadh but often visited her mother, to translate for me. She was an attractive and vivacious young woman in her late twenties. Bright and intelligent, she spoke very good English. Topics for conversation were family, weight problems, fashion and food. Husband and mother-in-law jokes were popular, if somewhat on the crude side!

Usually dinner is eaten with spoons and forks at the long, inlaid marble table in the dining room. *Eid* is a special occasion and a return to Bedouin roots. Silver platters of food are laid out on a large, plastic tablecloth on the carpet. I follow the guests, and as we began to sit down cross-legged on the floor, a well-built, large-hipped woman goes for the same spot; we collide and I go flying! I soon learn that the choicest places are near to the Princess, and so as not to compete, I find I have an easier time sitting lower down in the pecking order.

Settling myself, I see the eyes of a sheep's head staring at me! A whole sheep is served, in the traditional way, on an enormous bed of rice. Fingers, right hand only, are reaching in to break off pieces of roasted meat. The left hand is used to mould the rice into a ball, which is then popped onto a slightly extended tongue. I learn that when eating from a communal dish, fingers should never touch the mouth or tongue.

My neighbour breaks off a piece of the sheep's stomach and offers it to me. It is customary to pass the choicest morsels to guests or other eating companions. It is impolite to refuse. Trying to look appreciative, I manage to swallow it, quickly taking the taste away with a glass of Coke. Along with the eyes, brains and tongue, the feet are also eaten but are rather gooey in substance. Not the sort of food to eat in a designer dress.

Saudi cuisine is high in animal fat and sugar. Influenced by other Middle Eastern countries and the West, Saudi varieties are growing. Traditional meals are meat and rice dishes, *kabbza*, lamb or chicken cooked with onion, tomatoes, rice, cardamom and other favourite spices. Vine leaves and peppers stuffed with meat and rice are especially delicious, as are various bean dishes.

The breaking fast meal is after *maghrib* – sunset prayer. The popular choice of food is *shurba*, a thick meat and vegetable soup eaten with *sambusik*, triangular pies with a spicy meat and onion filling. *Laban*, a yoghurt drink is also a favourite.

The cooks in our household are cooks, not chefs. Of Turkish and Egyptian origin, they have learned by experience and are rather rough and ready. The food is too greasy for me, and the vegetables overcooked. The Princess is especially concerned to order salads and fruit for me. As I grow to know Muma Fozia, the Egyptian cook, an elderly and formidable woman, she will often bake a fruitcake for me to have with afternoon tea. At every meal in the Palace the first group of guests make room for a second, and the servants and children are last. Leftover food from parties and banquets is sent to charitable organisations through the mosques.

The meal over, we all adjourn to another room for dancing. An all-female band arrives with a singer. The loud rhythmic beat, played on hand drums shaped like large tambourines, makes a strong, raw, primitive sound. The younger women and girls know the lyrics of most of the songs.

"Do you like our pop music?" shouts Princess Jowaher over the ear-piercing noise. Composed by Middle Eastern musicians from Saudi, Qatar, Bahrain, Lebanon and Egypt, the music is constantly played on television, radio and cassettes by the younger generation.

The female Arab dance is a sexy dance. Hips and legs move seductively, graceful arm movements give a subtle dignity. This is when the Saudi lady lets her hair down, quite literally. The 'long hair swinging dance' is spectacular, as luxuriant tresses are swung from side to side, round and round, in a frenzy of uninhibited pleasure. As the evening warms up inhibitions are unleashed, and the more expert performers are clapped and encouraged to express what must be their only truly creative outlet. No place for a man? A typical remark from an Essex husband back in England might be: 'Stop making an exhibition of yourself!'

After a short time watching I feel I have learned the basic steps and style. The beat of the music is irresistible. Moving towards the dance floor outstretched hands and delighted smiles draw me into the dance. A long scarf is tied around my hips. Cultural and language barriers disappear. I get a 'buzz' and a hint of what tribal unity is all about. Saudis do not see themselves as individuals as much as part of a whole family-tribe. Their responsibilities are to the group rather than to themselves.

When the music stops I am tingling with pleasure. As I take my seat my elderly neighbour speaks to me. Curious, I signalled to Princess Lamia to come over to translate:

"She is happy for you that you could dance the Saudi way, and share your happiness with everyone." The instinctive warmth and spontaneity, the lack of pretension of these women give me confidence in myself. I want to reach out to them in a reciprocal exchange. I hope very much that as time goes on we will all be richer for the experience.

Chapter Four

The Timeless Order of Islam

"Phyllis, you like the Muslim? You *can* - like *me* - say this."
Princess Sarah hands me a booklet written in English: *How to become
a Muslim.*

"Look," she points to some words on the first page: "Say
this!" I read aloud:

"'There is no God but Allah and Muhammed is his messenger.'
Is this your book, Sarah?" I am puzzled.

"No, it's from Ba-Ba's books. Ba-Ba teaches me in English."
She means Pa-Pa, Prince Muqrin. Arabs have difficulty in
pronouncing the letter 'P'.

So often I wait in her big sitting-room for her to finish the
asr, the mid-afternoon prayer. Then she can begin her studies.

"OK, you be the teacher: every day you teach me how to
pray, we need to practise." Her face falls. Nine year old princesses

have better things to do, watching cartoons on TV and playing with friends. I begin to recite the *Shahada,* the basic tenet of Islam. Taken from the *Qur'an*, it is written on the national flag and appears everywhere.

Arriving in the country where the Prophet Muhammed was born during the holy month of *Ramadan*, I am immersed into the *raison d'etre*, the very essence of the life of the people. The four weeks fasting, the breaking of the fast with family and friends, sending food to the mosques for people less fortunate, creates a sense of unity. This sense of community amongst Muslims is worldwide.

Day and night TV and radio relay the prayers said by tens of thousands of pilgrims - men, women and children - as they gather round the holy *Ka'aba*. The *Ka'aba* is the central place of worship in the holy mosque in Makkah, which God commanded Abraham and Ishmael to build over four thousand years ago. The site of the sanctuary was, Muslims believe, established by Adam.

Arabs trace their decent from Ishmael, Abraham's eldest son. Ishmael and his Egyptian mother Hagar were saved from banishment in the harsh desert by a miraculous spring of fresh water welling up from the sand at Zam-Zam. The tradition of this holy water is preserved in the Zam-Zam well in Makkah. Pilgrims and visitors to the holy city are welcomed with dates and containers of Zam-Zam water, which is also sold in the major towns throughout the month of *Ramadan*.

Circling the *Ka'aba* seven times, *tawaf,* to show love for God, symbolises Hagar's search for water between the Mountains of Safa and Marwah.

I plough through an English translation of the *Qur'an*, lamenting the loss in translation. The *Qur'an* has incomparably beautiful language; translations into other languages are no longer the true *Qur'an*, which is a record of words revealed by God through the archangel Gabriel to the Prophet Muhammed. Gabriel's revelation takes the form of *Surat*, verses describing man's relationship to his creator Allah. God's words were written on stones and palm leaves, and recorded by his followers, under supervision from the Prophet Muhammed during his lifetime.

Studying the holy book and religion dominates everyday life. Division between the secular and the spiritual does not exist. As soon as they can read children learn how to pray and to study the holy books.

By research and question and answer sessions I grasp the basic tenets of Muslim life, the five pillars of Islam:

1. *Shahada* - faith: only God is worthy of worship and Muhammed is his messenger.
2. *Salat* - prayers: which must be performed five times a day.
3. *Zakat* - charity: a Muslim calculates his/her own *Zakat*, usually a yearly payment to charity of two and a half per cent of a person's capital.
4. *Sawm* - fasting: by denying worldly comfort, even for a short time, a fasting person grows spiritually and learns sympathy for those who go hungry.

The fifth pillar of Islam is the *Hajj* - the pilgrimage to Makkah. Muslims are required to make this pilgrimage if they possibly can. Some people save for a lifetime to go. Sometimes a family or community will club together to send just one representative to experience the great moment when rich, poor, employer and servant - all are united before God. I found the whole concept deeply moving.

Pilgrims are obliged to wear similar clothes, so all stand equal before God at Makkah, the birthplace of Muhammed where God's will was revealed. Only Muslims may enter the city at checkpoints along the entry road. Pilgrims are asked if they are Muslim and must have documents to prove it or they are turned back.

No hierarchical authority exists in Islam, no priests. Prayers are led by *Imam*, learned persons who know the *Qur'an* by heart and are chosen by the congregation. No one has the right to make legislation that contradicts the *Qur'an*. To do so is to put oneself in God's place, thus committing an act of grave *shirk*: the sin of worshipping other gods besides Allah.

Islam is submission and obedience. The *Qur'an* reminds man the purpose of his life on earth is his duty to himself, his family, his community and his fellow human beings. More than a religious structure, Islam is an holistic approach to the world and to each aspect of everyday life. Manners, hygiene, social guidelines and family relations, business and politics, no detail is exempt from the moral principles of Islam.

At noon while shopping in a supermarket a few days after my arrival, suddenly the lights dim and I am aware of being alone. Nervously moving towards the cash desk I spot my driver waving at me from outside. I am locked in. It is a prayer time.

Businesses, banks, shops, close for half an hour three times a day: *zuhr* midday, *asr* mid-afternoon, and *maghrib* after sunset. The Palace has its own mosque, a house of worship serving the community in times of trouble and hardship, a centre for religious study, and a meeting place.

Women pray at home. I am getting used to the response: 'She's praying,' when I ask for one of the family, or for a friend to come to the phone. According to the *Arab News,* they may not go to the mosque 'for fear they will distract menfolk or be seduced'

To prepare for *salat* - prayer, Muslim women wash, then wrap themselves completely in a very large piece of lightweight cloth. When I share a room with Hanan, a Muslim teacher from Syria, I am amazed by the white apparition that bends and sways to low chanting in the very early morning. The divine law *Sharia,* that all things are accountable to God, is taken seriously.

I ask to see an image of Muhammed but mosques have no statues or pictures of him or his life in case people treat such things as idols and inspire blasphemy, therefore pictures of the Prophet can only be guesswork.

Mosques are not dull. Scarlet carpets, green brightly patterned tiles, marble pillars, huge chandeliers, intricate stonework and stained glass windows, symbolise what Islamic art is all about.

My driver Ahmed is deeply religious. He learns English by talking to me about his faith. Car journeys are often halted by the call to prayer. He teaches me to say: *insh'Allah* (God willing), and I answer expressions such as 'see you later', *insh'Allah,* a reminder of the belief that God takes care of everything.

On Saudi desert roads for drivers who have swapped camels for cars *insh'Allah* is not quite enough. Car accidents are frequent; the driving chaotic. Ahmed is careful but even so, I often feel anxious.

"No problem, Ahmed die," he says one day, grinning from ear to ear, his strong white teeth in a flashing, wolfish smile. "Paradise for Muslim nice - very nice - beautiful girls serve you - anything - everything! Nice - very nice."

'In Paradise I prepare for the righteous believers what

no eye has ever seen, no ear has ever heard, and what the
deepest mind could never imagine.'

Thus Hadith (also *Sura* 32:17).

Saturday is the first day of the working week. At home I like Saturdays, the beginning of the weekend. I never like Mondays, which are now Saturdays! Losing track of days and never getting into a regular daily routine, I have to be flexible and on my toes. At a moment's notice there will be trips to Jeddah, Riyadh, or to Prince Muqrin's farm forty minutes drive into the Nefud desert. Then lessons and plans are shelved.

I can mostly depend on the daily schedule from Saturday to Wednesday when I take the two princesses to their private school in Hail for 7.30am, and collect them again at 12.30pm. Ahmed drives us in the white Cadillac.

It is a charity school that donates a proportion of the fees. The children call it their desert school, an old white concrete building that needs repair. The dusty open-air courtyard has small classrooms, an office and staff rooms on one side, and a high surrounding wall like all houses and educational institutions in Hail, to protect females from being seen.

The old wooden door is locked and guarded by the female caretaker, a bent crow-like figure in black from head to toe. She waves a large stick at late-comers and naughty children which scares me until we exchange greetings and I realise she only *looks* sinister. Two male caretakers sit on the floor of a covered area outside and rickety stairs lead up to a second storey annexe and a few more small classrooms. The desks and chairs need renewing and the text books need updating.

In keeping with Muslim ways, Arab staff are friendly and welcome me. I find two English teachers, an Egyptian and Syrian woman, and I am greeted with kisses on both cheeks. We promise to exchange ideas and my spirits lift. I am lonely at the Palace.

Chapter Five
A New Semester

I am learning the etiquette of Palace life. I am not in control of my life. Eyes are everywhere. There are times when I feel like a goldfish in a bowl.

Like governesses of the past I am isolated. I am the only Englishwoman so I must sharpen my instincts and adapt to spontaneity, in keeping with the rhythm of Palace life. Islam's sense of community helps.

Yoga teaches that a balanced mind, body and spirit are healthy. I practise and meditate every day, taking my countless walks around the Palace gardens. I listen to spiritual music tapes and it puts my life into perspective to read and re-read the inspiring and courageous Aung San Suu Ky's *Letters from Burma*, particularly: 'While maintaining courage and humility, one should not abandon caution and self-respect'. When I can't assert myself as a woman, I have to learn humility, and be brave. I am fearful. Without my respect I would be lost. I wish I could help Aung San Suu Ky in her unjust imprisonment for democracy.

I swim in the ladies' indoor pool often alone. The palace ladies do not exercise. Under a high ceiling the oyster marble hall has comfortable sofas and armchairs, changing rooms each with bathroom, shower and sauna and in all this luxury, space and time, I long for friendship and love.

Telephoning home isn't easy. I need patience and luck to find a Palace operator who isn't praying, eating, or sleeping. Incoming calls are hit or miss. Private houses in Saudi Arabia have no postal delivery, mail goes to sponsors or companies. Women are not allowed into post office buildings in town. I am anxious for a stamp for my first letter home and I have no idea where to post it. The only post box seen from the car window is by the security gate in the men's quarters.

Even the simplest requirements, where to wash my clothes, trying to find the laundry room in a labyrinth of corridors in the basement of the Palace, is a nightmare and *then* the door is locked. I have memorised the security guard's telephone number. He is prompt and he is vital. Internal phones are everywhere, even in the lifts.

My letter stays in my pocket for days until I spot Princess Sarah's Filipino nanny giving a stamped letter to a Palace workman. She sells me a treasured stamp, bought for her by a Palace driver. The workman hurries off to post our letters, I have never in my life been so dependent on men!

A new semester has begun. The team of tutors assembles: Prince Bander, Princess Jowaher and Princess Sarah are royal children and they are required to shine in the class room. I am their personal English tutor, Hanan their personal Arabic tutor. Freelance Arab teachers visit the Palace daily from 5.00pm to 7.30pm, Saturday to Tuesday, at weekends during exam times. Homework has to be completed most nights and tests are frequent.

My three charges are not studious types. They are intelligent, bright, lively, with a great sense of fun, yes, but they study English at their parents' request, not because they want to.

Bander runs his own football team: Aja Palace. The strip matches the Saudi team colours: green and white. The football pitch is in the men's section and the only way I can watch a match is with binoculars standing on the balcony of the study room on the top floor of the Palace!

Football is a popular topic for English conversation classes. I turn Princess Jowaher into a TV interviewer – a female presenter is appearing on Saudi TV for the first time - and Bander is a player from the Saudi football team talking about the 1998 World Cup. The world's most popular sport has brought insular Saudi Arabia its first cultural breakthrough onto the world stage, the first national following of something happening outside their country; so we can talk football. But no footballer or singer becomes an idol. It is a grave act of *shirk* to idolise any human being.

Bander's essays are mostly about his diving adventures in the Red Sea, or his passionate ambition to become a pilot like his father, Prince Muqrin. My problem is Bander's talent for telling convincing stories to avoid study. His charm and teenage anarchy put me to the test and I step into my 'Headmistress' role... sometimes I win. I like Bander – round and jolly with his loud boyish laugh. He is direct, warm, friendly, he avoids every English lesson he can and his

English is not at all good though he is intelligent and he does complete a summer course I arrange for him at Eton College which makes up for all his pranks. He did ask Prince Muqrin for permission to come to London from Eton at the weekend. My advice was if he leaves the college he won't go back - so he stayed!

Princess Lamia takes me on a shopping spree to Riyadh, where I swan around the shopping malls buying more books and study resources. I persuade her to buy some tennis rackets. The girls need to get out into the fresh air. From an air-conditioned house, they get into an air-conditioned car to take them to an air-conditioned school – and so on.

I ask Princess Jowaher: "What is your favourite hobby?"

"S-L-E-E-P!" she replies. There is a great reverence for sleep in royal circles. When answering my internal phone in my rooms I am often greeted with the phrase: "Are you sleeping?" If I need time to myself, I answer sleepily, "A-a-ah. Mmmm- yes?" knowing I will be treated with the greatest respect.

Jowaher is a very good student and we build up a rapport, perhaps a friendship. She remembers grammar, pronunciation and new vocabulary. Petite and curvy she is a bit of a tomboy who can make the loudest whistle I've ever heard to her friends from the Palace balcony, and if her lessons are not interesting enough then I soon hear about it.

I adapt *Aladdin* from *Arabian Nights*, for her school class to perform at their end of term presentations. Twelve eager faces greet me as I hand round the scripts. With the help of Jowaher's teacher, Hala, we choose the most suitable girl for each role. I have brought my cassette player and a tape of Rimsky Korsakov's *Scheherazade* but as I plug it in Hala whispers in my ear:

"Phyllis – Saudi – no like music in girls' school." I look at her in amazement!

With all the courage of my convictions I reply: "Oh Hala...*do* let them hear this *beautiful* music! I have arranged a dance-drama as a prologue to the play." She looks nervous, but allows me to continue. I perform the steps and movements, for the girls to see what they have to do. Near to the finale the door slowly begins to open. The look on the headmistress's face is enough to tell me I am doing something wrong. She can't speak to me in English, she mutters something to Hala, who translates:

"The Muslim law bans music in girls' schools." I stop the tape. Eventually I use tambourines and find a large free-standing drum belonging to Prince Muqrin in a corner of the main guestroom on his desert farm. Jowaher receives permission from her father to use the drum which is duly transported to the school.

Right at the last moment Jowaher decides she isn't 'right' for Aladdin, and that she wants to play Scheherazade, whom she considers to be an extraordinarily clever woman able to remember one thousand and one bedtime stories, and outwit the Patriarch – a radical notion for an Islamic princess!

It is the first play in English to be performed in Hail. A primitive stage area is especially built with a curtain and a proscenium arch at the end of the open-air school courtyard. I am director, stage designer, wardrobe mistress, make-up lady, stagehand and technician. The girls know little English and in one scene the Djinn makes a nervous entrance *before* Aladdin rubs the lamp!

The school courtyard is full to capacity for the performance. In the audience is Princess Abtah and a Who's Who from Hail and nearby.

Hidden in the wings Hala and I, in Egyptian theatrical tradition recite a summary of the play. She translates into Arabic from my English all through the dance drama.

As I am leaving, the headmistress kisses me on both cheeks and presents me with a gold watch, Princess Abtah is all smiles, an excited Jowaher is much congratulated on her performance and the headmistress thanks me for helping in the school.

Female teachers in Saudi Arabia are mostly Egyptian or Syrian. Girls were not educated until the 1960s when King Faisal's enterprising wife Iffat set up a national committee for female education and slowly, against prejudice from religious leaders, schools began to open all over the kingdom. *The Guardian* has reported in 'Educated for Indolence' that female students graduate higher than males and only two percent of the 275,000 women graduates are part of the work force. Crown Prince Abdullah, the reform-minded acting ruler, is quoted saying he will allow no one, whoever they are, to undermine or marginalise women's active role. I know of three Saudi women teachers in Hail who have braved the restriction to the home rule.

Of my three pupils, the youngest – Princess Sarah, aged nine, is a little madam. She does her best to put me in my place and takes her position as a princess very seriously. Her beautiful, lustrous and large, dark Muqrin family eyes gaze at me directly and defiantly. Her one desire is to 'tell me what to do'. During her lessons I keep very calm.

After lessons we have fun together; dancing to tapes or singing Victorian music hall songs like *Daddy wouldn't buy me a Bow-wow*, quite relevant as Muslims consider dogs are unclean. Prince Muqrin would never have a dog in the Palace!

Princess Sarah gets very fidgety and restless and times her lessons on her wristwatch. "English" she says, "is not important."

We will see about that.

Chapter Six
Making Headway

Princess Abtah quickly wins my respect and devotion. I am sensitive to her tone of voice, body language and circumstances. She walks into my study room unexpectedly, not to spy, but she makes sure her children are taught as she wishes and are happy and making progress.

It takes a blend of dignity, diplomacy and decorum to control clashes, disagreements and tensions in my teaching situation. In Islamic culture conflicts are dealt with in a diplomatic, discreet way. Nevertheless, I speak my mind simply and directly to the children and to Princess Abtah.

Teaching is what I look forward to. I spend a great deal of time preparing lessons and I am disappointed and frustrated when Jo-Jo or Bander eventually arrive late and separately, or when no one turns up at all and I have to phone round the Palace trying to find out why.

I know their private Arabic lessons are from 4.30pm to 7.00pm and take up their evening time and energy. My lessons are from 7.30pm to 9.00pm so they are often very tired. I try in vain to change my lessons to times when the children are fresher. I suggest weekend lessons, or changing the time for Arabic studies. Their afternoon siesta has to happen and I am frustrated by the ancient culture and rhythm of life at the Palace.

It is entirely up to me to lay down the law regarding punctuality. I deal with absence from lessons as best I can and hunt out my elusive students, physically escorting them to the study room. Princess Abtah often assists me in this task.

The slow pace of life, the aura of calm and serenity, could easily lull me into apathy, so I make myself available all day every day. I cannot have a 'free day' because individual 'freedom' to do what *I* want, *when* I want and *how* I want isn't allowed to an English governess at the Palace. So I teach my royal charges socially, at lunch, at dinner, swimming, on a rollercoaster ride in the Range Rover with Bander driving over the Nafud desert dunes, or in the Palace gardens and corridors.

Twice a week Ahmed drives me to the impressive house of the Saudi Palace Administrator in Hail. Princess Abtah has asked me to help his daughter, Noff, aged seventeen. Noff has ambitions to become an English teacher. I am not offered any extra money.

Noff is pleasant but lacks motivation and quickly forgets. We walk round and round the small garden beneath the fortress walls of her house, the only recreation for Saudi girls, making English conversation about her friends, family and teachers at her ladies' college in Hail.

Her Egyptian tutors and I disagree over pronunciation and

grammar. Noff says: "We tell the teachers: Phyllis say – you wrong. They say: *we* right, *Phyllis* wrong!"

At Christmas time, I tell her about the Christian festival. She knows about the birth of Jesus, and Father Christmas. I explain the ritual gifts and family gatherings and how sad I am that I cannot celebrate with my family this year.

Before Christmas day, I arrive and she invites me into the best sitting room, an uninspiring place, furnished with heavy, dark wood furniture, dark curtains, goatskin rugs and large ornate framed wall plaques of verses from the *Qur'an*. To liven things up she puts on her tape of Arab pop music, phones up for a take-away pizza to be delivered, opens bottles of Coke and gives me a beautiful gold necklace.

"This – my Christmas present for you – Phyllis." We dance and twirl to the music together, mixing disco and Saudi styles, bringing life, colour and joy to the gloomy rooms and to Noff's first Christmas party.

The Dean of the ladies' college comes to see *The Arabian Nights* at the princesses' school. Desperate for opportunities I pass a message to her and although things move slowly in Arab culture eventually, after hassling on the phone, I am invited to the College; a shoddy building, drab, and without colour, posters or paintings. Stares and excited chatter greet my arrival, groups of girls peer at me around corners. I discover I am the first English woman to come to the College, which was opened in the '80s. The only communal space available is a large area, with white painted concrete walls and floor, which is used by the students for coffee and tea breaks. It is full to capacity with students and teachers.

Putting my notes on a rickety table, I see a megaphone ready for me. With voice projection, and student participation I give a talk about English teaching methods.

The girls are genuinely pleased, eager to speak the English they study for a teaching Diploma, though only a small percentage succeed. The youngest are seventeen and I notice a few pregnant ones but here early marriages happen and births do not interfere with studies because most Saudi families keep servants.

I offer to adapt *Romeo and Juliet* and *A Midsummer Night's Dream* for a College presentation. As Juliet defies an arranged marriage and *A Midsummer Night's Dream* deals with the supernatural, both taboo subjects in Muslim culture, and music is not allowed, I am limited in what I can do. They are wary of the West and want to preserve their culture.

Previous royal governesses were not allowed to meet the local community at all. Apparently my predecessor was dismissed for jogging round the men's Palace, wearing a leotard and complaining continuously she was bored and the Royal Family were 'a load of clodhoppers.' She wandered round the gardens reading *Alice in Wonderland* aloud. I know how she felt. And the royal command: 'Off with her head' is not a fantasy in this country.

Chapter Seven
The Desert Farm

"Hi Phyllis, we go farm." Princess Abtah telephones in her sexy contralto voice. I look forward to the Wednesday afternoon flurry of excitement as cars are packed and last-minute instructions given, before we speed out towards the Nafud desert. A convoy of People Carriers is leaving for the weekend visit to Prince Muqrin's farm: princesses, friends, ladies of the Palace, nannies, servants, cooks, dressmakers *et al*.

A cultivated desert is truly astounding. Water is precious. Average rainfall is less than one hundred millimetres a year. The Aziz farm is irrigated with recycled water-sewage and artesian wells. Crops are wheat, dates, fruit, vegetables, olives and nuts. They say 'spit on the desert and a flower will grow'.

When rain falls families pile into cars and head for the mountains, to gaze with wonder as waterfalls cascade and dry lakes gradually fill up with water. After days of heavy rain Prince Muqrin took Princess Abtah and the princesses into the Nafud desert to see the flowers which had sprung up everywhere and I was touched when Jowaher returned with fresh bright yellow and white flowers for me.

I ask permission to use Prince Muqrin's library on the farm. The National Commission for Wild Life Conservation and Development was established in 1986 (1406 AH) and has created eleven wildlife natural reserves that cover about two and a half percent of the country, and plans exist to create one hundred and two areas.

Encouraged by water, Arabian oryx, *reem* gazelle and *idm* gazelle, bustard, ostrich, crows, black kites and sparrows thrive in the kingdom. The oryx was saved and leopards, wolves, foxes, antelopes, baboons and jackals roam.

In *Wild Flowers of Central Asia*, Betty A Lipscombe Vincetti lists more than eighty wild flowers in regions thought to be barren. The desert grows acacias and desert shrubs, salt bushes, tussock grass and cacti. Fertile regions boast date palms, apricot, lime, quince, grape vines and vegetables.

Princess Abtah loves the farm. She and I take long walks in the cool of the day under shady date palms, through orange and lemon groves, peach and apricot orchards. Silence is broken now and then by the bleating of a sheep or a goat, or the singing of a skylark overhead. The Princess confides that it is at the farm, away from the formality of Palace life, that she completely relaxes with her husband and children.

The *ummah* is the one big family of Islam and loyalty to family is the foundation of Islamic society. Home is far more sacred, creative and rewarding than any place 'outside'. The culture is based on kinship, and 'family' includes remote members of a common tribe.

Family ties are ingrained from childhood and take precedence over any other obligation or relationship. Young men educated abroad usually return home. Often three generations still live under one roof.

In Muslim families grandparents take precedence, children are taught to be respectful and considerate. It is unthinkable to pass over the care of the elderly to a stranger, they are nursed safely into the next life. Eighty year old Muma Hasna, an African woman who was Princess Abtah's nanny when she was a child, has her own room in the Palace and a personal servant.

I walk to the farm boundaries where the warm red colour of the Nafud desert stretches out before me. Beyond the sculptured and sensuously curved dunes, black mountains rise dramatically from the sand. Birds of prey wheel across them, suddenly swooping to snatch a lizard or hare.

I begin to learn to value silence. Desert people know the art of listening. In the vast, infinite, awesome space they develop a profound sense of being, and hold themselves still in the presence of God. Balzac spoke of the desert as 'God without man'.

The Aziz farm takes its name from Prince Muqrin's father, Abdul Aziz bin Saud, who, in 1932, united the tribes of the Arabian peninsula and founded the Kingdom of Saudi Arabia.

When Prince Bander tells me his grandfather's life it sounds like a *Boys' Own Paper* adventure story. Smuggled out of the country in *his* father's camel's saddlebag at the age of twelve to exile in Kuwait he spectacularly returned with forty warriors to restore the family fortunes in 1902.

Abdul Aziz was a fearless, charismatic warrior. In thirty years he created a government where none had existed before, winning battles, marrying and divorcing twenty wives from other desert tribes, and begetting forty-three sons and uncounted daughters!

The discovery of oil in Dhahran in 1938 miraculously changed obscure desert existence into a phenomenally wealthy country. Abdul Aziz was a legend in his own time. Prince Bander tells me his grandfather's body was covered with battle scars when he died in 1953 and, wrapped in a white unseamed cloth, he was buried in an unmarked grave.

Abdul Aziz was succeeded by his son Saud, who abdicated in favour of Faisal, a much revered and respected king who continued to build the country in strength and solidarity. His plans included education for girls (for the very first time) and improved housing and health care.

Princess Abtah rings my bungalow:

"Phyllis…come; come cook for Princess Lamia, please."

Flour, butter, eggs, baking powder, jam, cream, and an improvised cooling grid are found and I demonstrate in a noisy crowd of talkative ladies and children how to make scones with cream and jam. I explain by miming the English tradition of 'tea-time'. Princess Sarah on her highest horse interrupts:

"OK, OK..Yes, Mama and me have tea at the Dorchester Hotel *every* day in London."

I extol the wonders of pudding in English cuisine and wish later that I hadn't, as exhausted, I furiously beat the batter of a Yorkshire pudding, put finishing touches to a bread and butter pudding, and prepared fruit for a summer pudding.

Eating takes up a large part of the day when we are at the farm. A Bedouin style open fire is lit for the evening meal in the landscaped garden beside a large, ornate fishpond and sprinkling fountains. It is here I taste for the first time grilled camel steaks which are delicious and low in cholesterol, and locusts, which I do not care for but are high in nutritional value: John the Baptist survived on them. Hot rounds of bread are served from the farm bakery.

On winter nights the temperature falls below freezing. Princess Abtah, the princesses, relatives, friends and children sit inside the huge, black, goatskin Bedouin tent. A roaring fire blazes in a fireplace with an outside chimney. Servants are sent to fetch fresh goats' milk, which is boiled and served hot with ginger in small, handled glasses. Marshmallows are toasted and *baklava* pancakes are a sweet snack. Dates, the ceremonial offering of welcome, are always offered and Princess Abtah, who knows their high nutritional value, teaches me to eat them dipped in the yoghurt drink *laban*.

I can sometimes persuade the princesses and cousins to perform a short improvised play, or a female group of musicians blast the tent with piercing dance songs. The party goes on into the early hours but I am tired by foreignness and the effort I put into each day to survive. 'Lights out' for me in the bungalow is 10.30pm.

At Christmas a Christian in a Muslim country sees blue, cloudless skies, temperatures in the seventies, and it doesn't *feel* like Christmas:

no winter weather, no big advertising campaigns, no pressures to buy cards and gifts. But as Christmas day draws near, I enjoy not being forced to celebrate the god Mammon!

"You make – the Christmas, Phyllis, like English – on the farm, OK?" Princess Abtah says when I mention the festival.

So Ram, an Indian farm worker, and two of his colleagues and I move the furniture out of my bungalow. The essential simplicity of Christmas is poignant so near to where Jesus was born; I want to celebrate for religious reasons. Surprisingly I find a turkey in the deep freeze of a local supermarket. It roasts slowly in one of the farm ovens for the Christian servants and myself while I teach the princesses, cousins and friends Scottish country dancing. Whirling and twirling, they love the rhythm and pace of the taped Scottish music. They learn the *Gay Gordons*, *The Dashing White Sergeant* and *The Hopscotch Polka*. They are wide-eyed with enthusiasm, but they lack Scottish stamina and soon fade like desert flowers exhausted on the floor.

My Christmas festivities end in the chill desert night, round an open fire, under a velvety, midnight blue, dazzling starry night sky. In this part of the world the stars are intense and glow like lamps in an unpolluted sky. It doesn't take long for everyone – from Ethiopia, Syria, India, the Philippines, Sudan, Kenya and Pakistan – to learn to sing with me and the young princesses songs they had never heard before, like *Jingle Bells* and *Away in a Manger*. It is a treasured time of peace and goodwill amongst people of different nations.

Chapter Eight
A Bedouin Family

"Come Phyllis – we go Bedou!"

I grab packets of crisps, biscuits, chewing gum and a large cake, hoping the Bedou family will accept these gifts – they are all I have to give at the moment. Outside the door I remember the golden rule for visiting the desert: my water container.

One of the Palace Saudi telephone operators, who has worked in America, is to drive me out to a Bedouin encampment. I have been telling Princess Abtah of my wish to visit a Bedouin camp, and have not been at all satisfied with her usual response – *insh'Allah*.

The Bedou are the true desert people and their hospitality is legendary – it is a tribal duty for them to offer protection for three days to anyone who needs sanctuary, even a declared enemy.

"Princess – good woman – what she ask – Abdulla – he do," Abdulla tells me in respectful tones as I climb into the Range Rover.

He says only a few Bedouin still lead a nomadic life. Most of them have been lured away to the cities – bribed by financial settlements from the government.

In the back seat of the Range Rover I keep my head and face covered. A woman travelling on her own in a car with a man who is not a blood relative can be stopped and questioned by the *muttawa* – the religious police. I hold my breath! Thankfully after a few miles the Bedouin camp comes into view. In the cool, early morning Spring weather my cheeks are burning with excitement.

Our arrival causes a flurry of excitement. As we drive up, the women, seeing a strange man, cover their faces and disappear swiftly into a tent followed by a child, crying loudly. Three small boys stand transfixed in their tracks, their fresh young faces full of curiosity. I hold out my gifts to the boys, which are received with bright eyes and smiles, showing strong, white healthy teeth.

Men appear swapping salutations with Abdulla and shaking his hand warmly. They move towards a tent, Abdulla calls to me:

"Phyllis – we drink coffee – come." I am the only woman in a group of five men. I feel privileged to be invited but uneasy, knowing Saudi customs regarding women. Gingerly I walk into a large and roomy tent.

A welcoming open fire burns in a grid on which the *dallah* – coffee-pot – stands warming. Nearby an older man with a grey beard sits on a threadbare, brightly coloured carpet, playing an instrument rather like a primitive cello with the same mellow tones. A slim, good looking man settles down on some cushions and reclines like Valentino to light a cigarette. He gestures to the older man:

"He – Mr Sheraidy – grandfather – he play Beethoven!" Peals of laughter ring around the tent. I begin to feel at ease.

My romantic dream of meeting desert nomads is not to be. To find a traditional nomadic tribe I will have to travel many hours into the heart of the desert. Here we have the urban *Bedou*, who speaks a little English, goes shopping at the local supermarket, and takes his children to school in the Toyota truck parked outside.

His camels, however, have not become obsolete. I have seen two standing placidly by a water truck, which pipes cold water to taps for washing and cooking. Abdulla tells me camels are far more reliable than a truck and indispensable to the Bedouin. They provide meat, milk, cloth woven from the coarse hair, and belts, saddles and water-skins are made from camel skin.

The traditional three rounds of coffee with dates are served. Still not accustomed to the added cardamom, I gently wobble my cup after the first two, as a signal that no more is required.

Mr Sheraidy continues playing, now singing in sad, soulful tones. I ask Abdulla to translate the lyrics for me.

"He play the *rebabah*." This ancient Bedouin instrument is made by hand from wood with three horse hair strings. The bow is also made of wood and horse hair.

"He sing about his three wives – the last nineteen years – and the *only* girl he loved – who dead."

At the end of his song, Mr Sheraidy wipes tears from his eyes with the end of his *ghutrah*. He doesn't speak English, so as I got up to leave I ask Abdulla to seek permission for me to shake Mr Sheraidy's hand. It is not customary for a woman to offer her hand to a stranger. I have read of the hard, simple, noble and poetic life of the Bedouin and, greatly moved by what could be the last generation, I want to pay my respects.

Mr Sheraidy insists on giving me his *rebabah* which I shall always keep, I sincerely hope he has another one. To my surprise he also presents me with a baby goat, which unfortunately I *can't* take back with me!

The wonder of the desert has entranced me and I want to know more. A few weeks later I eagerly accept an invitation from some American friends of the Royal Family who are visiting Aja Palace, to accompany them to an ancient archaeological site in the far north of the peninsula, at a place called Jubbah. Permission to visit the site has been given by the general director of museums and ruins in Riyadh.

The road through the desert to Jubbah is long, straight and seems never-ending. Occasional small communities of undistinguished cinder-block buildings are dotted along the way. A flock of vultures distracts us from looking out for wandering camels – a hazard on the road which causes many accidents.

Our first port of call is the local constabulary, where we present our papers and are introduced to our police escort. With the usual courtesy and kindness the Chief of Police invites us to take coffee, mint tea or ginger tea, with the members of his staff in his large office. Settling into a comfy armchair, I know we will be there for quite some time: Arab hospitality is never rushed.

A bumpy drive over scrub takes us to the site to meet the local guide Muhammed. His old weather beaten face is deeply lined.

Walking with the Ramblers Association in the UK has prepared me for an event like this: I feel smug in my sensible walking shoes as I scramble easily over the rocks. Cries for assistance come from the two American women, their long *abayas* getting in their way. I have heard about western women breaking bones and badly bruising themselves, even ending up in hospital, all as a result of wearing these long shapeless garments to which they are completely unaccustomed.

I too have experienced an embarrassing moment in a supermarket when my shopping trolley had to be turned upside down to extricate the end of my *abaya*, which got wrapped around the wheels and was dragging me down!

It is late afternoon in April, the temperature is getting hotter as spring turns to summer, and I am glad of the higher, cooler altitude. Muhammed has stopped in front of some stunning red-coloured rocks. Cameras click to record fascinating prehistoric carvings of human figures with shields locked in combat, of ibex, gazelles, inscriptions in ancient script, etchings of wheels and, most remarkable of all, longhorned cattle which have not been seen in Arabia for thousands of years. I am taken back to a culture which existed over four thousand years ago. It makes me feel humble and as significant as a grain of sand.

We return to the farm which is a godsend, an extra dimension in my closeted existence, and teaches me to love and respect the desert. Even there the heat is unbearable and I wait until late afternoon for fresh air – and then look for a shady spot. My favourite place in late spring is to sit and read under a huge mimosa tree by a pond and waterfall in the farm's landscaped garden. Glorious yellow mimosa flowers cascade down and cover me completely in a glowing canopy.

Chapter Nine
Journey to Jeddah

Ahmed impatiently sounds the car horn outside. I zip up my weekend bag. He doesn't like to be kept waiting for a governess! We join the convoy of cars as they sweep out of the heavily-guarded Palace gates and onto the airport road.

We are on our way to a Royal Wedding at the late King Khalid's Palace in Jeddah. Security guards wave us through the airport entrance and the cars sail past VIP signs and pull up by the steps of a private jet – a new treat for me!

The charming Saudi air hostess welcomes me aboard in English. She settles me into a luxuriously comfy seat and fastens my gold-plated seat belt. Glancing around I see gold plate everywhere. In the bathroom I turn on gold-plated taps to wash my hands.

The moment we are airborne exotic fruit cocktails are served, and a smart steward wheels round a trolley covered with delicious sandwiches and mouth-watering fresh fruit. Next come hot lobster and chicken.

The ladies are lively, chattering about the most important event in an Arab woman's life: her wedding day. Marriages are arranged by parents. The integrity and stability of the family is the first goal of Muslim society, so marriage is a contract between families of clans not between individuals.

I have talked to several would-be brides. Courtship and engagements are western customs. The girls always accept a proposal because they love their parents and Islam and still accept the traditions they have been brought up in. Sometimes a girl is fortunate enough to have a look at a photograph of the betrothed and one young lady I met was even allowed to speak to him occasionally on the telephone.

"I saw him from my window!" a delighted girl told me.

Their first meeting is on the day of the wedding celebrations, *walimah*. The wedding contract or *nikah* is not sacred but a binding business contract, giving husband and wife rights and responsibilities. It pre-dates the celebrations by months, even years. The terms must be recorded with a *Qu'adi* – the judge and witnessed by two competent adults. It stipulates the amount of *mahr* – dowry to be paid by the husband to the wife. It's her money to give a bride financial security and she can use it as she sees fit, in theory anyway.

Islamic women do not take their husband's name but keep their own identity to emphasise the status of family and lineage. The *Qur'an* says a Muslim woman, single or married, is an individual in her own right, with the right to own and to dispose of her property and earnings.

Islamic law allows a man up to four wives. A woman I meet

in Hail shares her wealthy husband with three other wives. The women live in a house of their own with their children. Some less wealthy husbands share the same large house. One or two wives seems to be normal.

Not being allowed to have male friends in this country I do not know how men really behave to women – they certainly do disappear to countries where alcohol and women are part of the culture, and then come home again. At one birthday party I go to, all the women are dancing around happily until one of them is told, "Oh – your husband's here". I am astonished to see her cheerful expression change to real terror, and she runs fast to get her *abaya* to 'cover up'. The Prophet's instruction for couples is that a woman should only be married to a person who is good enough or compatible enough for her – *Hadith* – and *'The most perfect in faith amongst believers is he who is best in manner and kindness to his wife.'*

Some months before the Royal wedding a Lebanese designer who goes to the Paris, New York, Milan and London fashion shows, comes to design clothes for Princess Abtah at the Palace. Before leaving she says to me: "You have nice dress too?"

"Nothing *special*," I reply. I feel rather out of place.

Later Zahara, Princess Abtah's personal servant, brings a beautifully hand-embroidered *kaftan* to my room and I recognise that it belongs to *Amira* – I remember admiring the way she looked in it.

In Saudi culture showing admiration compels the recipient to offer the object of delight as a gift to the admirer. A gift of a pair of shoes straight from a lady's feet after a compliment of mine taught me to practise a little tact, or to smile refusal so the person who offers you the gift does not lose face.

All modern Saudi royal brides own a video of their wedding and Lamia commissioned a Lebanese musician to compose music for her grand bridal entrance. The video lasts for hours, a Who's Who of royalty that captures a lavish extravaganza and celebrates a couture-clad, dazzling, radiant bride performing like a movie star. Watching it I get to know at least the faces and names of the Royal Family I work for.

Newspapers never carry stories or pictures of the Queen and Royal princesses. The desire for privacy in Saudi culture, especially in Royal circles, means marriages are never publicised, and perhaps to control the dynasty, are privately arranged, often between cousins, or within the Royal Family network.

Permission is required to take a photograph in Saudi Arabia, for fear the image will be seen by a man. I am never allowed to photograph Princess Abtah or the Royal children. Jowaher and Sarah love snapping each other, and their cousins and friends, and paper the walls of their bedrooms with the pictures. Life-sized photographs of the Royal Family adorn the royal apartments and banqueting halls instead of works of art, with wonderful pictures taken by Prince Muqrin of his falcons swooping down on their prey, and hares racing away in the desert, hanging beside prints and photographs of green fields and flowers, streams and lakes and trees.

Royal Saudi ladies keep busy social lives. They visit each other's residences in Riyadh and Jeddah, and their local friends. They attend weddings and go to functions at hospitals and schools. Only male royals perform public duties and attend state occasions reported in Saudi and English language newspapers.

We fly for an hour and I can read the *Arab News* and the *Saudi Gazette*. Another treat! As we descend I can see a lagoon and harbour on the Red Sea. Will I be able to bathe in its biblical waters? The jet lands and the usual flurry of excitement begins as servants and nannies jostle to get out and into waiting cars. After Princess Abtah and the princesses speed away it is a 'first come, first served' exit. I usually end up squashed between large-hipped Muma Fozia, the Egyptian cook, and Fatima, an overweight Sudanese woman – and it happens again.

At the Jeddah residence I share a room with Hanan, the Arab teacher for the royal children. Hanan speaks little English, goes to bed very late after chatting with the ladies of the household half the night and unsettles me with her prayers: *salat-al-isha* – between darkness and dawn and *salat-ul-fajr* – between first light of day and sunrise.

She is in her mid-thirties and her favourite English words which she repeats often are: "Hanan – look – husband." She will have to wait until she goes home to Syria. Unmarried couples who socialise publicly in restaurants or shop together are breaking local morality laws and can be jailed or deported.

We are in the south west of the peninsula and mid-April is hotter than in Hail. Unpacking my *kaftan* I reckon it is not every Englishwoman who is invited to a Saudi Royal Wedding.

The day of the wedding, Princess Abtah's sitting-room looks like a beauty parlour. No hairdressers or beauty salons are visible on the streets. A mobile hairdresser and beautician work in the client's home or vice versa. A manicurist paints *Amira's* fingernails and her face is immaculately made up. A wispy delicate gauze veil covers her head and floats on her shoulders. I have never seen anyone look so dignified in curlers!

It is 4.00pm and the *walimah* begins at 10.00pm. I am used to waiting patiently for something to happen. An hour later Jowaher turns up in her *abaya* with her best friend Shou-shou, Muma Hasna's granddaughter. They are best friends with Shou-shou's two teenage sisters. These girls love Arab Pop music, and copy western style fashion as much as they can.

"Phyllis – hurry, we go to Corniche." Jowaher sweeps down the huge marble staircase. I grab my *abaya* and hurry after her, pleased about a diversion. We pass the vast expanse of King Fahed's Palace overlooking the sea on the Corniche road which runs for seventy five kilometres along the Red Sea. The sea and space and Africa on the horizon lift my spirits - a wedding is a hard call for a widow.

"Oh, can we stop? Can we walk by the sea?" The girls look at me as if I am mad. A group of young men are swimming and fishing. Women, covered in their *abayas*, sit on carpets on the pavement near the rocky shore segregated or with their families. I *have* to be down on the shoreline, to take in the fresh sea air, to go where I want, when I want. We stop at a small chic café, and sit in the 'ladies' section. I am restless. I sit down and get up again.

"Excuse me Jo-Jo, I'm just going for a walk." Jowaher looks worried, but before she can say anything I hurry out onto the Corniche, pulling off my head covering and shaking my hair free. As I begin to walk car hooters blast at me. I feel a burning heat, not from the sun but from MEN staring. A car slows down beside me, cassette player blaring, young men laugh and wave at me – I feel hounded like an animal. One of them leans out of the window:

"Bitch!" he shouts. Shock. Tension in my neck and shoulders. Fear. My stomach muscles contract and my legs go rigid. I can't go on. The royal car pulls up beside me.

"Get in, Phyllis, get in!" shouts Jowaher from the car window. She is very anxious, safe inside behind the tinted windows.

I say "How stupid. I should have known better." It is true. A woman doesn't walk in the streets alone here. It is dangerous.

From the car I watch modern sculptures spectacularly displayed against sea, trees and neat shrubs, fantastic high buildings and plush exclusive hotels. Jeddah is the gateway to Makkah, which gives it its cosmopolitan air - religion has made Jeddah the principal shopping centre in the Saudi kingdom.

As I absorb the scene I try to calm my mind. How long can I live like a prisoner in a gilded cage, with occasional wild break-outs? I am missing John and I am missing England.

Just as our journey ends we pass a wonderful marble mosque, its vibrant blue dome reflecting the constant colour of the sky. The sight soothes me, and puts me in a better frame of mind to enjoy my first Royal Wedding.

.

Chapter Ten
A Royal Wedding

Hanan and I are waiting. To be able to 'sit and wait' is a fair part of my job and I practise it as a challenge and a skill. Hanan's a formal woman, with black oddly penetrating eyes. She stares at me in a way I find rather sinister in her brown wool ankle-length skirt and matching button-up jacket, red leather court shoes with small heels and her hair pinned back in a bun at the nape of her neck. A medallion engraved with *Qur'anic* verse hangs off a long gold chain and, unlike the other women, she does not wear any scent.

It is ten o'clock.

Walking towards us from her room I see Princess Jowaher.

"Jo-Jo…you look stunning!" I really mean it. She is wearing a long beautifully-designed princess-line silk gown in a delicate shade of apricot made by her favourite designer, Valentino. Delicate lattice pattern, long gold classical Arabic earrings adorn her ears.

"What's *stunning* mean?" she looks puzzled.

"I'm stunned, knocked out, amazed," I mime astonishment opening my hands and holding them up and drawing in a breath, "at the way you look – you're a knock-out!"

"Yes…yes…I know…" pipes up Sarah punching the air in my direction, "bang…bang…bang…knock out!"

The best English lessons are social ones.

"Y'allah!" – let's go. Princess Abtah walks with the posture that makes her appear every inch a royal princess. In the Palace office they say she is like the Queen of England. Today she does look wonderful dressed in a black silk brocade jacket and ankle-length slimline skirt. Her necklace of large red rubies and diamonds dazzle my eyes. Ruby and diamond earrings gleam against her lustrous, blue-black, immaculately styled hair.

Arab children mature early and Jo-Jo looks elegant, comely and mature at fourteen years. Even Sarah looks grown-up in her white muslin flouncy dress with red bows and a red topknot hair ribbon.

Muslim men and women celebrate marriage in separate ceremonies. The men gather for a grand dinner after *isha* prayer and leave early. The women's wedding party is a festival with music, dancing, singing and at royal weddings, a banquet.

We are on our way.

A hundred or more Rolls Royces and limousines block the grand driveway entrance to King Khalid's Palace. As usual security guards in green berets and khaki check each carload of guests and wave them on to park.

I follow Princess Abtah and the princesses joining what look like a flock of blackbirds descending on a garden full of glow-worms.

The huge Palace gardens are lit up like fairyland. Candles burn on all the small round tables covered with black lace cloths. Tiny coloured lights decorate the trees. The night is still and humid and this lavish scene is set under a blue-black velvet sky.

Before my eyes a transformation takes place. Black robes come off to reveal the seductive, the sexy, the elegant, the overdressed, the beautiful, and the vulgar.

Four hundred princesses and their relatives and friends are here tonight. In Saudi Arabia there are twelve thousand royal princesses.

Jewellery sparkles on their ears, throats, fingers, arms and in their hair, as brightly as their wide pearly-teethed smiles. Hollywood's Zsa Zsa Gabor must be their role model!

Long black hair sways over plump bums. Perfume wafts by me as the women pass.

It is a glittering affair. Bosoms and cleavages and bronze bare legs are on show with slinky gold and silver lamé dresses. WOW! I am astonished … and not a man in sight!

A raucous ladies' band strikes up. Sexy ladies dance with sexy ladies, their hips swinging, their hands twirling to the gutsy vibrant beat. Ladies sit together, stand in groups together, wander around together, gossip together and eye one another…a glitzy fashion show. Dressed up children run naughtily between tables chased by distraught nannies. Waitresses in black suits with long skirts, fifties black court shoes, hair tied back in dark gauzy scarves, and no make-up, parade around offering guests crystal goblets of mineral water on silver trays. Dates and chocolates sit in silver dishes on each black lace tablecloth.

I have lost track of Princess Abtah. Feeling strange and out of place I sit down at the nearest table, next to a lady wearing the popular gold lamé dress. She has a sophisticated air about her.

"Excuse me," I begin, "where is the bride?"

"She'll be here at twelve," comes the reply in excellent English with a slight American accent. I am relieved to meet her. Haifaa is a Saudi whose husband lectures at Harvard University and their son is at public school in England.

A western woman is never lonely for long amongst Muslim women. I feel I have known her all my life. Haifaa remarks how slim I am.

"Saudi women are always trying to diet. I'm cutting out salt and sugar." She pushes a large bowl of chocolates out of reach with a sigh.

The waitresses are on parade again, this time with highly-coloured drinks on the silver trays. I sip fruit cocktail through a multi-coloured straw and close my eyes and in my imagination taste Dom Perignon champagne. Delicious!

The band stops. Light flashes in the distance. Haifaa stands up. The official photographer is taking pictures of the bride's arrival.

I quickly walk behind the band, through the trees, to a vantage point nearer to the bright carpet laid for the bride to parade up to the steps of the Palace. *Muzak* plays softly. Giant viewing screens in the garden relay her entrance like a rock concert.

Here she comes, an Arabian princess, the granddaughter of the late King Khalid, on her wedding day. Young, demure, a little uncertain of herself, her cream veil over her hair and shoulders but not over her face, wearing a princess line, long-sleeved, high round collar, simply cut, cream silk dress with her beautiful long black hair woven in strands of jewels and pearls. She carries a bouquet of huge white trumpet lilies.

Two small dark bridesmaids follow her, overdressed in frilly short Shirley Temple numbers and wedge-heel black leather shoes.

The bride has never met her bridegroom before and, not being used to appearing in public and undoubtedly a virgin, the evening must be an ordeal for her. Lamia tells me at her wedding she was so nervous her legs shook when she faced the hundreds of people but Saudi princesses are accustomed from early childhood to parading down long rooms to present themselves and they walk with lovely poise.

I see the bride walking alone on the purple carpet as long as a church aisle and up a grand flight of steps to take her seat in front of the Palace.

Close family come up first to kiss her. The two radiant mothers fuss with her veil and pose for photographs. Guests, all women, one by one come up to greet her. The garden buzzes with excited chatter and the giant screens relay 'The Bride Show.' An extravaganza!

Suddenly our attention is alerted again: enter stage left a group of men, striding out, *ghutrahs* and robes flying. The young bridegroom comes up the steps with his father, father-in-law and his brothers and they present him to his bride for the first time.

He takes his elevated seat on the throne chair next to her. In haphazard fashion family and guests go up and repeat congratulatory kisses. The two mothers are having a great time hovering. They are the stars, so proud to get their children married off each to a socially desirable spouse.

I hear the shrill sounds of *zaghareet* for the first time: an ululation created by rapid vibration of the tongue against the back of the upper teeth while holding a high-pitched note, an Arab woman's vocal expression of delight and joy. The *zaghareet* signals the departure of the couple and they are escorted to a car to drive to their new home.

The bridegroom throws coins to children and he presents gifts to his and the bride's family. His mother-in-law is given jewellery or cash in return for unveiling her own face to him!

On the following morning the bride-groom offers his wife a special gift – *subah* – of gold or jewellery to commemorate the wedding.

A firstborn usually appears within a year of marriage. Saudis consider childbirth a special gift from God. 'May you have many children,' is a common blessing and five or six children is usual. Saudi men take pride in virility.

"My husband like too much – me have baby," says Ma-ha, the wife of a Sudanese Palace driver. "I like go teach ladies in Hail – no like stay house all day." Ma-ha is employed by the government to teach women to read the *Qur'an* and to learn to write. Illiteracy among Saudi women is fifty-one percent.

The band strikes up again. It is 1.30am. My eyelids feel heavy and I am hungry. I pass the time until 2.30am walking round the garden, sampling expensive perfumes in the opulent ladies' room, and talking to a nanny from Scotland who is also wearing an expensive dress she admired on her employer!

Lamia beckons me.

"We're eating now…follow us."

Crowds of ladies surge into a vast magnificent room lit by chandeliers. Long marble tables are covered with a delightful selection of food from different cultures: Italian, French, Chinese, Middle Eastern. Fresh fish, vegetables, salads, fresh breads, exotic fruit, a dessert table – a truly royal banquet.

I mingle with the crowd and help myself to the delicious choice. People sit at small tables laid with cutlery and bottles of sparkling apple juice. No one speaks English at my table and I am embarrassed when I choke on a very hot chilli hidden in a salad. A coughing fit is not a pleasant experience in strange company...I hurry to the ladies room.

Overwhelmed and not used to eating in the early hours of the morning, I am so tired and I am alone.

I need peace, quiet, sleep.

Where is Princess Abtah?

She telephones Nasr the driver for me. Bright-eyed and obviously enjoying herself, she says she will stay, as is the custom, until *salat-al-fajr*.

At the exit gates to the car park I wait not very patiently for Nasr and watch ladies leave, covered once again in their black robes.

I believe these hidden women have strong characters and intelligence...so much potential...a silent power.

Chapter Eleven

Riyadh

There is a cold and formal air about Riyadh, the Wahabi homeland. The *muttawa* patrol the shopping malls and markets with their chastising sticks for the disobedient; sometimes they ride in cars with loud speakers to make sure that shops close promptly after the *muezzin's* call to prayer.

Princess Abtah often visits Riyadh. Her sisters, brothers, and Lamia live near Prince Muqrin's enormous, elegant residence by the city centre, a fortress with walls which peer unblinking at passers by.

On my first visit there I meet *Amira's* American friend Gabby from Los Angeles. She is lively and engaging in her late forties and has stayed on in Saudi Arabia after she and her husband stopped working at Prince Muqrin's farm. She kindly arranges with one of the drivers to take us on a tour of the city. Swinging out of the security gate onto a wide, tree-lined highway, I am disappointed at the dreariness, the sameness of the architecture. Flashing neon lights glare on shop fronts and traffic is continuous, flash American cars speed by a few mud brick dwellings next to towering office blocks, a modern water tower, and the elegant embassies.

Ali, the driver, stops at a small, secluded public park with walkways under trellises of rose and jasmine and sculptured fountains.

"Women can walk here," Gabby reassures me. "It's a park for people who work in the embassies."

Parading round inside the high security walls yesterday I craved the heavenly unpolluted air in Hail. Riyadh is stifling and on windy days fine sand blows in from the desert and stings your cheeks and eyes. I want to stay but Gabby is off to *Al-Manahil* centre for women, before it closes for lunch and the siesta break.

What an eye-opener that is! The only centre of its kind for women in the whole of Saudi Arabia. It has a timetable and programmes in Arabic and English offering swimming, body-conditioning, Yoga, aerobics, stretch and tone and dance classes for adults and children with tutors principally from England, Australia and America.

There's a beauty and hair salon run by ladies from the Lebanon. The British Council are sponsoring English Language classes, I see a large restaurant, gift shops, a waiting area with long low brown sofas and coffee tables on a polished floor, and a café. "This is a wonderful place…I must book some classes" I think to myself enthusiastically, completely forgetting the one big obstacle: how to get there? In Riyadh the royal drivers are always busy, women can't travel in taxis, walking is dangerous…frustration isn't the word for how I feel.

Government ministries line King Abdul Azis street - Ibn Saud's famous cubic palace built in 1936, and the *Qasr al Hamra* Palace built in 1953 by King Saud for the Council of Ministers.

Saudi Arabia is ruled by a king but it is not a monarchy in the western sense. A chosen son of Abdul Aziz and then a grandson is King, Prime Minister and Imam leader in prayer and religious matters. The Crown Prince is the first deputy Prime Minister, advised by the Council of Ministers, many of whom are members of the Royal Family. It is an autocratic Islamic monarchy moderated by a tribal system of hereditary Sheikhs, religious leaders and extended royal family.

Majlis al Shaura, the Consultative Council formed by King Fahed in 1992, has a Council President and sixty members selected for a four year period by the King from a cross section of professional men all over the country.

The official Saudi emblem is a palm tree over crossed swords – the palm symbolises vitality, growth and prosperity; the swords represent strength and justice – used by members of the Royal Family whether or not they hold ministerial positions.

Thirteen provinces each have an *Amir* (Governor) and local advisory councils. Prince Muqrin is the *Amir* of Hail province. The youngest son of Abdul Aziz, he is apparently charismatic, dynamic and accomplished.

One day I am having lunch in the kitchen/diner with Princess Abtah, Lamia and the princesses and the phone rings. Lamia answers it, repeating the message: 'Three Bedouins are at the Palace gate.' Prince Muqrin has recently come home from London after an operation, and the Bedouins have travelled for three days to give thanks for his recovery and to pay their respects.

"Come, Phyllis," Sarah jumps up, "come and see." We hurry to a large balcony overlooking the Prince's Gate and its grand entrance. Seated majestically on their camels, three Bedouins are making their way towards us.

Gabby insists on taking me to what she refers to as 'chop square'. Dira Square is where executions take place in public outside the *Amir's Qasr-al-Hukm* (the Emirate Palace) and the *Qasr-al-Adl* (the Palace of Justice).

Public executions!

I read that *Sharia* is the legal framework of Islam, derived primarily from two sources; the *Qur'an* and the *Sunnah* – the latter is an example of Muhammed's deeds and approvals concerning social matters. *Sharia* places the rights of Islamic society over the rights of individuals, who are judged as parts of the whole. The accused remains innocent until proven guilty.

In civil and criminal proceedings a *Qu'adi* acts as judge and jury, though the defendant has the right to appeal against the *Qu'adi's* decision. Legal costs are not recoverable. Interrogations are carried out in Arabic with translators provided when necessary – vital for a statement to be signed by the accused as correct.

Murderers and rapists are publicly decapitated. More than three thefts are punished by amputation of the right hand. Apparently thieves who steal from hunger and poverty are not charged. Adultery gets death, the act proved by testimony from four eye-witnesses. Minor penalties are public flogging, jail, fines and deportation for non-Saudis. Foreigners who travel in a car with a person of the opposite sex or consume alcohol can sign a paper swearing not to commit the same offence again. Women charged are not released until their husbands or sponsors collect them.

Dira Square is a horrible, chilling place.

At the Bedouin *souk* or antique market, an Aladdin's cave of treasures spill out onto the pavement from dilapidated lock-up shops: daggers, muskets, incense burners, coffee pots, camel saddles, a copper studded Zanzibar chest, vast silver platters, old silver, Bedouin jewellery.

Eighteen kilometres north of Riyadh a winged lion looks down on us as we pass under the crumbling arch of the entrance gate to *Dir'iyah*, the old walled capital.

We are the only tourists that day and it's an eerie climb up the dusty, decayed steps between ruined mud-brick homes that once kept people cool in the heat and warm in cold weather. At the top Ali stands between two ornate unsteady pillars and with the sun slowly setting behind him, he cups his hands to his mouth:

"Allah akbar – Allah akbar!" God is great, God is great. His prayer call rings out over the date groves and fruit trees below and the sand beyond, and he smiles: "This holy mosque – Mohammad ibn Saud – Sheikh – Dir'iyah." He is a Muslim.

Prince Muqrin is in Riyadh for an all-male cultural festival. Apparently there is singing, dancing, poetry and music from all over the peninsular and lectures by Arabic scholars. Prince Charles is among the two hundred dignitaries who watch in an auditorium behind bulletproof glass. One and a half million visitors are expected – no women – we watch on TV, Lamia, the princesses and relatives and me eating Chinese takeaway. We see the *ardhah*, a traditional sword dance performed before battle and Prince Charles joins in this dance. Swords are raised and in a long line sway ceremoniously to a deep rhythmic drum beat.

"I'd love to be there. Can no women attend?" I mutter.

"Now women can – this year a 'ladies day' – for women only," says Lamia.

I want to watch the famous camel race. Over a hundred camels are ridden by boys as young as eight years old for big prize money. After the camels a man throws his arms around aggressively and speaks in a loud rhythmic way.

"He say poetry about fighting," Sarah says. The power, beauty and range of Arabic create one of the world's greatest literary languages. Poetry and eloquence are revered in Saudi culture.

Territories, fights over grazing areas, water holes, desert roads, blood feuds, famous warriors and tribal battles, are all recorded and described in poems that become fiercely competitive wars of words for the desert Arabs.

The evening before Jo-Jo, Sarah, and their three cousins had sat huddled round the television, spellbound, watching an attractive young man in front of a male audience, reading from a manuscript. His face showed emotion which is rare for Arab men.

"Hela want marry – *him*!" squealed Sarah, putting her finger on the face of the young man on the screen. The girls giggled. Hela is eighteen, at the prestigious King Saud University in Riyadh. Fortunately she could live with her family because women who study in Riyadh or Jeddah cannot live alone on the campus.

There is strict segregation of the sexes and in the few departments for women all teachers are female. It is even difficult to get access to libraries. Hela gazes adoringly at the TV screen.

"Who is he? What's he doing?" I ask

"He is Prince – my father know him – his family. Look!" she clutches a beautifully bound book. "He write – he write poetry."

"What's his poetry about?" I take the book from her, used to opening an Arabic book at the back and reading from right to left.

"This – love – this – the nature, this – the life," she is wildly enthusiastic about him but she will never meet him unless one day they *do* get married.

Chapter Twelve

A Delicate Situation

By the two week *Dhu-al-Hijah* holiday at the end of April, days are long, hot and endless on the farm. Fighting lethargy I set my alarm for 6.00am to enjoy the cool morning. By 9.00am it is too hot.

My favourite walk is by the olive trees down to an artificial lake. Ducks and geese see me coming and squawk in the silence. I wish Prince Muqrin still fished from the jetty. A small, dilapidated rowing boat is moored and even in the desert scrub, water does refresh my spirit.

Past the peacock enclosure, the goat, sheep and camel enclosures, the vast greenhouses and the poultry coops, a farm truck sometimes passes but I see no one. I am the eccentric Englishwoman awake at that time of the morning – nobody else will stir before 10.00am.

I hide in the cool of Prince Muqrin's library to catch up with my reading about Saudi Arabia, if the two security men at the door tell me he is not there. Or I try to lure Bander and Jowaher away from joy-riding round and round the farm in their Range Rover to come and study with me.

Visitors come from Riyadh and Jeddah and at last one interesting woman, Princess Hannah, in her early thirties, married to Faisal, the eldest of Princess Abtah's four sons. Quite tall and formal, she is close to her mother-in-law and I discover when I admire a still life painting in oils hung in a dining area, that Princess Hannah is the artist. She only realised she could paint when she helped one of her three daughters with her art for school. She experimented by herself, found an art teacher in Jeddah, and her work has been exhibited there. Princess Hannah has promised to introduce me to Safiya Benzagar, the Saudi artist whose work is apparently an inspiration for Saudi women.

One of Princess Hannah's unmarried sisters, Saha, in her twenties, joins the princesses and me for a game of tennis on the floodlit courts in the cool late evening.

"Why? Why 'Love'? Why?" Sarah can't understand. "What it mean?"

Scoring our game turns into an energetic English lesson and Sarah storms off because no one is hitting the ball to her. Jo-Jo was up late the night before and is too tired, so Saha and I play.

"I try tennis – Jeddah – but no like ladies play tennis," Saha tells me. I hate the soaring grasshoppers and the attacking mosquitoes but I volunteer to play with her every evening, jumping at any chance to bring something to my pathetic social life.

In these undemanding days and afternoon siestas I think about a small but for me desperately important pilgrimage of my own.

My sons, Richard and Jason, have bought a handsome sailing trophy to commemorate John. At the end of May there will be a presentation and a memorial service at the Island Sailing Club in Cowes on the Isle of Wight. It seems unthinkable not to be there but I am not due for a holiday until July. In the Arab traditions of duty and loyalty relationships can be ruined by pushing too hard – it is a delicate situation if I want to keep my job.

I shall telephone my younger son Jason – who had sent me an invitation to his passing out 'wings' ceremony in June and I must be there. If he writes to me and sends a covering letter from the Sailing Club, I can read it all to Princess Abtah. That should do the trick.

Post can take fourteen days. Censorship can delay anything. A package I received had the breasts and lower parts of Henry Moore's *Mother and Child* sculpture blocked out!

Jason's letters arrive. Timing is crucial. Princess Abtah is always at her best around noon when she likes to relax in her day sitting-room before lunch, and to see the children back from school. While the princesses change clothes I take a deep breath and read the letters to her.

No response.

I emphasise the main points of the letter again, slowly and clearly. Her face is serene and expressionless.

"How long you go Phyllis?" I swallow. Can I really stay any longer here? The food, the cockroaches in my kitchen, my sudden frustrated urges to go where I like, when I like, and how I like. I miss freedom. Plays, concerts, conversation, calling a friend, changing a library book, most of all walking alone in the street.

The silence stretches until she breaks it by saying gently:

"We go London – in June – come London house and after –

come back to Palace with us."

I am so relieved all I can manage to say is: "Thank you, Princess Abtah," and I hurry to my room to call Prince Muqrin's office. *Amira* has already telephoned and instructed them to book me a ticket to Heathrow.

I sit at my table and weep.

Freedom again…I can hardly believe it will come true. Nearly every minute here is a strain, obeying Arabic codes of behaviour, practising obsequiousness, with no intimate friendships, without my family. I've walked for miles, inside the garden walls, along the Palace corridors, on the farm, repeating to myself: "I need the money…I need the money…"

Chapter Thirteen
Thoughts on Departure

Bander, Jowaher and Sarah have revision and extra tuition for the end of year school exams with their Arabic tutors after the afternoon siesta. There's no time for English lessons. I pass the Arabic study room one evening and a tall, dark stranger walks by. He doesn't acknowledge me, that is the custom, but there is something about him.

He is Muhammed, headmaster of a boys' school in Hail, Bander's tutor who teaches Jo-Jo history and maths with a female servant in the room. In fact he is a Saudi professor. He intrigues me. Oh well. I am leaving.

"See you in London," kisses and hugs from Rahma and Nafisa when we have our last Turkish coffee in their room after lunch. Every servant wants me to buy something. "Phyllis – go London," and pointing to a garment, "This – buy – OK?" Sandals, vests, tights, T-shirts, scarves, cotton skirts – an endless list.

Immigrant employees send wages home for their families. Rahma's widowed mother struggles alone in Eritrea to educate three children. Rose, the seamstress from the Philippines is divorced and educates her son at college. Rita, Sarah's Filipino nanny has three children under ten to feed at home because her husband was killed in the civil war.

Rita is my chaperone when I go with Ahmed and his wife to the mountains to look at lakes and waterfalls after the heavy spring rain. The Range Rover gets stuck in deep sand in an off-track area. Ahmed, perspiring and flushed, tries to dig us out, his efforts rewarded with adoration and cups of water from his wife.

An hour passes. The temperature is dropping.

"I walk to road track…there."He points to a desolate area.

We women huddle in the Range Rover. High hostile mountains enclose us, a rocky, sandy and inhospitable environment surrounds us.

Rita begins to tell stories she has heard of desert nomads kidnapping foreign women who were never seen again. The intimacy of our situation prompts her to tell me passionately about her longing for children and how she often cries herself to sleep at night.

"Two year – no visit – soon I go" Immigrant employees have to work for two years before they get a two month break.

A Toyota truck comes into view, Ahmed sitting in the back. Luckily three young men on a desert ramble spotted Ahmed. It doesn't take long for them to free the wheels. Shouting loudly to the men through the open window Ahmed starts the engine. Curious as to what he is saying I ask him to repeat it in English. "I say push…backside…more…more…push backside!"

Ahmed sometimes asks me if his English is good enough to be 'Driver Elizabeth the Queen?'

Back at the Palace Sarah runs out to greet us, flushed with excitement.

"The police – look for you." I push open the huge bronze doors and Jo-Jo runs down the long flight of stairs and hugs me.

"Phyllis – come – tell us everything!" My story is told again…and again…and again. Nothing much happens in Hail.

"Waa-Hoo! Waa-Hoo! Waa-Hoo-Waa-Hoo!" Bander's call echoes. This is his home from school greeting. *Amira* calls back in a lower tone. Sarah has a more successful bellowed greeting - a tribal family greeting all through the enormous palace. Lunch after school is in the kitchen. Servants follow us at a second sitting. Bread, *tahini* – sesame seed paste, *hummus* – creamed chick peas, *fattoush* – tomato, pepper and cucumber salad dressed with garlic, parsley, mint, olive oil and lemon and *tabouleh* – cooked burghel wheat with tomatoes and onions and a mint, parsley, oil and lemon dressing. Lebanese cuisine at least has won my heart!

Bander surveys the table from the opposite end to his mother.

"Where's *kabbzah*?" It is his favourite meal. A servant phones Muma Fozia:

"Send *Kabbza* for Prince Bander."

He turns to me: "Phyllis, you go today. I sorry – I – miss you." I am astounded. Bander always does his best to avoid me.

I have survived for five months. I look out of the window, out over the Palace walls to the desert.

Getting in and out of Saudi Arabia is not simple. Exit visas are required to leave the kingdom. I have asked the Palace office for mine but I get the usual response *insh'Allah* – if it is God's will!

I stand outside my rooms. It is 4.00pm and the plane takes off at 5.30pm. Where is Ahmed? I sit on a garden bench out of the scorching sun in the shade of a leafy date palm – one of my favourite resting places. In late May the garden is glorious, full of pink and white roses, giant marigolds, scarlet, cerise and purple tropical flowers and the music of the fountains making water patterns in the air.

Mixed feelings of sadness at leaving such serenity and beauty together with excitement at the prospect of what is waiting for me fill my head. Being part of an extended clan holds me together, giving me the much needed security and comfort for the grief I feel for the loss of John.

The *salat-al-asr* prayer call between afternoon and sunset rings out from the Palace mosque. Ahmed swerves the white Cadillac round the flower beds and stops beside me. My stomach gives a lurch. Oh no! He will have to pray…has he got my air ticket, my visa? Will I ever get away?

At Hail airport I shake Ahmed's hand: "*ma'salaamah*."

He gives me his wolfish smile: "See you – September."

"*Insh'Allah!*" I reply.

In the women's section of the airport lounge I feel conspicuous. I am wearing only my *abaya*, not my veil and face-covering like the other women. I see their eyes and their heads move – to peer at me.

On the hot tarmac I am tingling with excitement at the thought of being in control of my own life again.

The flight prayer is said...we are airborne.

"You know why they put their women in bin bags, don't you? Because they're bloody clever, that's why...To my mind they could take over, given half a chance."

I sit next to a Londoner who is on his way home from working in Saudi.

"Can't stand the place," he goes on, "can't wait to get down to the pub. They keep an eye on you too. My mate got caught making a lovely brew. He sold it to a Saudi...big mistake. He got a flogging and deportation...nasty business."

Derek is the first Englishman I've had a conversation with in my own language for five months. Chatting to him brings me back with a thump to all that is familiar, my own language, culture...my family. Tears burn the backs of my eyes. I'm going home.

London

John's memorial is wonderful, joyful and sad. My experience in Saudi is only a bridge to a new life. I am not over that bridge yet and I know I have to go back.

It is late June, rainy and not very warm. Clouds scud across the smoky, grey sky. The phone rings. I hear Princess Abtah's voice.

"What you do, Phyllis? We London – come to house."

Maybe I *am* looking forward to being with the Royal Family again. Their London home - how do Saudi Arabian ladies behave in the West? How does a royal entourage from an enormous palace fit into a London house?

My taxi stops in front of a three storey Georgian house close to St James's Park. Rita, Sarah's nanny, is standing on the front steps chatting to Bernice, Princess Hannah's youngest child's nanny who has Lou-lou in her arms. Omar, the Turkish 'dogsbody' is putting the rubbish out.

I imagined luxury but the entrance hall is stripped of carpets and furniture. In the sitting room, all I can see are two canvas chairs, and ladders propped against the walls. Princess Abtah is sitting on a packing case against one of the walls in the hall; she does not look happy. My "how are you?" receives a sharp response.

"Don't ask. They not finish – slow – all house get new." Princess Abtah uses the words 'don't ask' when she wants to dismiss whomever she is addressing.

Omar carries my luggage upstairs to an attic room. I am a governess again. We climb the stairs, stepping over paint pots, rolls of carpet and servants squatting on the stairs waiting to be called. Two single beds take up the whole space in a very small room, an arm's length between them. The only piece of furniture is an inadequate, dilapidated wardrobe. The carpet is worn out, the curtains need cleaning. All the other rooms are occupied; I am the last to arrive, and I get the worst room. Pushing my suitcase under my bed I feel hard done by, badly treated. What am I *doing* here, anyway?

Loud snores and mumbling in a foreign language wake me from a deep sleep. A woman's form in the other bed lies near enough for me to touch. Growing accustomed to the dark I catch my breath…Oh, no! The one woman in all the royal household who makes me feel uneasy: who watches me with staring, searching eyes that bulge out of their sockets; whose large and awkward body always squashes me on car rides; who speaks her mind in a crackling tone through gums that boast only a few brown teeth. Yes, it is Muma Fozia, the Egyptian cook.

I pull the bed-clothes over my head; tomorrow I will buy ear plugs.

My alarm wakes me at 7.00am. I dress hurriedly from my suitcase. I have to get Jo-Jo and her favourite cousin Shuroq off to their English course, in a smart English Language school overlooking Green Park. Getting her out of bed is not easy. I open her bedroom curtains and am ordered to draw them again and again, before I SHOUT at her in my loudest voice.

The course is daily for six weeks and Jo-Jo forecasts they will not survive the first week but with perseverance, encouragement from me and their growing confidence they see it through. I want Jo-Jo and her cousin to use the bus and experience everyday life in London but time is always against us so we end up going by taxi. It is strange to see the girls go out of the door without their *abayas* in jeans, sneakers, T-shirts, jackets and jockey caps.

After lessons they always prefer to walk home, clearly revelling in the freedom of ambling along the street and mixing with young people from other countries – Russia, China, Japan, Korea – college definitely broadens their outlook. When a Certificate of Merit arrives from the language school she is very surprised.

Jo-Jo has a Korean pen-friend and takes her letters to school to read to her friends in Hail when she gets home. Bander only corresponds with students from the Eton Summer school if they are 'female, blue-eyed, blonde and Nordic' (his words to me!). I am sure Bander can charm the birds off the trees!

Prince Muqrin took Bander to Eton and met the tutors, saw round the College and had a cup of tea in Bander's room. Princess Abtah went with the Prince to look at Windsor Castle and I think they were impressed. Jo-Jo and Sarah got as far as Big Ben but the

Trocadero in Piccadilly was where Jo-Jo and her cousins spent most evenings.

The Saudi Royals are fond of England and the English. When Prince Muqrin was a young man in the Royal Air Force College at Cranwell, he trained as a pilot and Princess Abtah lived nearby in a country village to be with him – their two elder boys were babies – then they bought a London house, within walking distance of St James's Park and Hyde Park.

For me, London parks are the most imaginatively designed and best cared for in the world. Now, living in a claustrophobic atmosphere and a crowded house with no privacy, escape to Hyde Park is an absolute blessing. I stroll about remembering when I was a girl at the Arts Educational School, a stone's throw from Marble Arch. The park was our back garden, and whenever we could escape from a heavy timetable of school work, ballet, drama and music lessons, we would swim in the Serpentine or take out a rowing boat.

Back in Saudi the servants gossip about what is regarded as immoral behaviour between the sexes in the London parks: "I see…together …lay on grass…do like the dogs…bad… no good people."

In the London house interior designers and mural artists begin work. A husband and wife team fly to and fro from Paris. Ceilings in the best sitting-room and dining-room become cloudy skies, *Amira's* favourite kind of weather. Pillars are marbled, wall panels wood-grained.

It is a chaotic household. The only familiar scene is Muma Fozia's kitchen, which looks as if it has been transported lock, stock and literally barrel from Hail. Large vats of rice, *kabbzah*, *shurbah*

– soup, and *waraq anyab* – vine leaves, with Muma Fozia watching hawk-eyed, surveying her kingdom. She still makes me nervous.

I feel as much a fish out of water as I do in Saudi Arabia. Here the servants close ranks in the cramped quarters. They are insecure and defiant away from the Palace life. I am an English governess again: a survivor, set apart, stoical, tolerant and resilient.

Princess Abtah and Princess Hannah shop with a passion. They spend days looking for curtains, carpets, paintings…art treasures. They love the sales, getting up early to catch the best bargains.

In a shop in Bond Street, Princess Abtah collects a dress that has been altered.

"What name?" she is asked.

"Abtah," the Princess replies.

When I arrange Bander's summer course at Eton she tells me, "No Prince – say Bander Muqrin – OK Phyllis?"

The royal women do not cover their heads. They dress modestly in ankle-length skirts and long-sleeved jackets, even in hot weather.

How Muslim women dress in the West is determined by the male head of the family. I see shrouded women in segregated groups sitting on the grass in Hyde Park, or walking with a male family member.

The Edgware Road appears to be transformed into a new Arab state. Arab men sit outside cafés smoking hubble-bubble pipes, *narghileh*. Food shops smell of Arabian spices. Shelves are stacked with dried chickpeas, beans, pulses, pitta bread, Arabian coffee, dates, rice. White *thobes* hang side by side with black *abayas*. *Qur'anic* verses shine on gold and silver plaques. Arabian lutes,

The Palace. I am on the balcony of my study room.

All covered up for my first shopping trip with Ahmed and Nasr, the
palace drivers.

The palace garden at night.

Princess Jowaher in her *abaya* waiting to go to school with Rita
(Sarah's nanny) and Linda (Jowaher's nanny).

Myself and Mr Sheraidy outside his Bedouin tent in the Nafud desert.
He is presenting me with a baby goat as a parting gift.

My first attempt at camal riding in Jeddah.

Out on the desert farm. Prince Muqrin owns all the land as far as the eye can see.

The effects of heavy rain in the desert. Taken on the trip with Ahmed and his wife just before getting stuck in the LandRover.

oudes, hand-made mats, bags, medallions…Apparently Arabs like to come to London to get away from the heat.

Princess Hannah takes me to a party games shop. I am to arrange a traditional English children's party for the princesses, cousins and friends who are in London for the summer. Her Rolls Royce draws up in front of the house. An impeccable well-mannered chauffeur, Norman, opens the door of the car for us – a contrast to Ahmed. Norman *suits* expensive cars – he is the perfect accessory!

Swanning around in a Rolls is new to me – so *very* English, and what superb comfort and performance. I could quite safely drink a cup of tea at thirty miles an hour and not spill a drop.

We have our English party. Mothers, aunts, friends and servants play blind man's bluff, musical chairs, pass-the-parcel and dancing lions. Arab children love to cheat in games and can't see the point of fair play – a headache for any party organiser!

I have hired a room in a local Leisure Centre and decorated it as best I can, with the help of Princess Hannah. Red, blue, green and yellow balloons hang in bunches between red and white streamers. Shocking pink and lime green Chinese lanterns, silver mobiles of fish and aeroplanes, swing from the ceiling.

Arabian food - layers of lamb, beef or chicken cooked on a rotating *shawarma* (gas machine) carved and served in pitta bread with a sesame sauce - is brought in from a take-away in Edgware Road. There is rice cooked with pine nuts and sultanas and stuffed vine leaves, *halva* for the sweet.

Five little princesses mime Spice Girls' tapes to loud applause, and we are having great fun, when I catch sight of Bernice sitting alone, looking downcast. I walk over to her:

"Are you all right?" I wonder what has happened.

"No – I worry – Rita run away at night." Tears well up in her eyes. "She no say where go – where?"

Royal nannies live isolated lives. They so much look forward to being together. They are each other's family. I know how she must be missing her friend, and I have heard about how the freedom in London and New York is sometimes too much of a temptation for Saudi employees.

The house begins to take shape. I can cook for myself under the menacing eye of Muma Fozia, but I no longer eat meals perched on a stool in the kitchen. Period furniture has been transported from Paris and I now sit at an impressive dining table. Around me are the rich vivid colours – reds, browns, gold, yellow, purple, silver, scarlet – of the sumptuous furniture, carpets, wall coverings and drapes.

"Flashy, very flashy," the delivery man comments to me as he looks around. "Not my cup of tea. *Turkish* are they? Yeah – they like a bit of glitter don't they?"

"You like come Italian restaurant, Phyllis?" Princess Abtah, Princess Hannah and lady relatives pile into the Rolls. We are off to a chic restaurant in Bond Street.

"Aperitif, Signora?"

What is expected of me? I *like* to start a meal with a drink. The waiter gives me the wine list – there is a deathly hush.

"Wine, signora?"

I *enjoy* a glass of wine with a meal. Nobody says anything. I feel the room is looking at me. I decline. If only I was fluent in Arabic I might explain that wine has for centuries been drunk as a celebration of Holy Communion.

Planning outings in London for the Royal children is a nightmare. The young princesses argue about where we will go. They love adventure playgrounds and Pizza Hut, the movies and McDonald's. No museums. I did manage to get Sarah and her cousins to the Museum of Moving Pictures, the children told Mr Hanif a movie director on a film set made them act out a scene in front of a camera. Amidst the hassle and excitement and with the language problem I had not told them it was 'make believe'. In fact, the small girls were naturals. They acted a few lines from a script of *The Adventures of Tom Sawyer*, learning the words off by heart and were highly delighted they were movie stars!

The most exhausting trips are to Regent's park. All the staff come for the outing. A convoy of cars travel the short distance – which would be quicker to walk. On arrival, the clan manage to get to the nearest park bench to sit, eat ice creams, chatter and watch the children in the playground. Apart from the ice creams, we could have been in the Palace gardens in Hail.

I ask Sarah: "Do you know the Underground?" Her face looks blank. "We're going on the Underground today".

Five glum faces look at me, aged from six to ten. We get to the tube station without too many complaints. The ticket machine, the automatic ticket gates, the escalators, the trains whizzing by in the tunnel, astound them. They love the Underground map I give them trying to pronounce the station names we pass. The day is probably their biggest adventure in London!

I take Jo-Jo and her cousins to Kew Gardens by tube. They have the map and I pretend that I don't know the way. They get lost but we get there eventually. At Kew Gardens they are horrified at the miles of grounds to walk in and with long faces insist we go home.

We take the boat trip back to Westminster Pier to calm my frayed nerves, and I show the girls the River Thames. Swans glide by the boat and I try to mime and tell girls that my grandfather was a Thames Watchman who rowed the Royal Swanmaster up the river in uniform to mark cygnets in the ancient annual ritual, 'Swan Upping.' In fact, on the embankment by the Globe Theatre a ferryman's seat, carved in a stone wall, has been preserved where my great grandfather, and his father used to sit waiting to ferry passengers across the river. As we sail down the Thames towards Westminster pier, by the looks on their faces, I believe I've captured their imaginations. Then I try to tell them about the renaissance the river will have for the millennium.

Princess Hannah sees *Grease* and wants us all to go, the princesses, cousins and myself. The girls can't understand much dialogue, but I watch them looking sideways at each other and giggling 'Oh – he fantastic!' Sexual relationships and freedom are another world for young Saudi ladies.

Princess Hannah wishes to study charcoal drawing and improve her English. Most courses are booked but I enrol her in one in Camden. After the first session she says:

"I no like Rolls Royce - students – people – look at me – what bus number – Phyllis?"

Good for Princess Hannah. I admire her confidence in herself and what she can achieve. The Saudi ladies I meet mostly watch television and gossip to relatives on the telephone.

How will Princess Hannah like her restricted life, after a spell in the west? Lamia says to me:

"Oh, we're used to it, we just adapt." Is it that simple? There's a veneer over their feelings which I know I cannot penetrate.

"Phyllis, please go – your house. No beds here – family, friends come."

Princess Abtah's request is a welcome relief. The bliss of living in my own home.

But then, when I hold in my hand a hammer, or some pliers from John's tool-box, and he's not there, and I have to try to do these things that he always did for myself, I am so frustrated by my own helplessness, and missing him and I stand in the garden shed, paralysed by my own powerlessness, in floods of tears.

In September I am back in London, getting into a large luxury coach with all the Royal staff piled in. The entourage is returning in the Royal Family's private jet to Hail. I am attached to this family and their ways. It is a privilege to be part of this complex fusion of the old and the new, and I haven't yet come to terms with myself, my loss, my future. I need to go back.

Chapter Fourteen

The Unhappy Return

"Phyllis – we land – come on!" Jo-Jo's voice wakes me, excited chatter fills the plane. Out of the window there are the black mountains, Jabal Shammar and Jabal Salme towering above Hail, that I see in the changing light every single day I live in the Palace. I have meditated on their beauty – an escape – away into the 'other world' beyond the Palace walls.

Unfastening my seat belt I think it won't be as difficult as it was five months ago.

"Where your *abaya*, Phyllis?" Sarah demands in her high-handed voice. Hurriedly searching in my grip bag, I sigh.

Where is my toaster? My cassette player? My ironing board, my kettle? The locks have been changed for security on my doors. The rooms, curtains and carpets have been cleaned, smelling fresh and welcoming. But the domestic appliances I slowly acquired have all disappeared. I am upset. I telephone *Amira's* sitting room: no reply. I telephone Jo-Jo.

"Ma-Ma gone Lebanon." Jo-Jo tells me Prince Muqrin has taken a short holiday after an operation in London. Only Bander, Jo-Jo and Sarah are here. Gabby, *Amira's* American friend often said to me: "Nothing gets done when Princess Abtah's away."

"How can I replace all my home comforts with your mother away?" I rant and rave to Jo-Jo after our lesson. I am shut out and fed up! She seems to grow a few inches taller – she literally rises to the occasion before my eyes:

"Make a list, Phyllis, I will give – Ali – he buy all – I get money from office." Jowaher instinctively takes over from her mother, she possesses the same managerial qualities, the same unpretentious authority. I am impressed. Two weeks later she says, "Phyllis – Ahmed take you to supermarket, he pay with money I give for you, buy all you want for ten days – Bander, Sarah and me go Lebanon."

I am going to be left with a few servants who do not speak one word of English. The royal car flashes by as I sit on a garden bench. Sarah waves jubilantly from the open window – she will be missing school! Sudden departure is part of the royal lifestyle. I have to be flexible with a big 'F'.

The azure sky, the paradise garden do not lift my spirits, I feel despondent, neglected and left out. I would like to stay in a luxury hotel by the sea in Lebanon, to see another Middle-Eastern country. Hanan has gone.

Autumn brings the date harvest. Ladders are propped against

date palms in the Palace gardens, large baskets lie at the foot of the trees. It is 3.00pm and the cleaners have come on duty after lunch and siesta. I wave to Smiley, a young Bangladeshi who cleans my rooms.

Twenty year old Smiley's smile stretches from ear to ear. He does things for anyone who asks him, smiling. I am used to the servants now but I still refuse to have a personal servant, someone waiting, watching, hovering around.

One phone call to security brings electricians, plumbers, TV engineers, carpenters, workmen from India, Bangladesh, Pakistan, Sudan, Philippines. The service company is in a compound outside the Palace walls. A light bulb, a blocked sink, TV channel adjustments, mice to catch, cockroaches to spray – all performed with polite civility.

The afternoon and evening stretch before me – What am I going to do for ten days? Jo-Jo has told Ahmed: "Take Phyllis – where she want – go." But where to go? The supermarket? Where else? I turn to Jane Austen. Her satirical humour always cheers me up and even more so now that I can see parallels between Austen's ambitious mothers in the claustrophobic, parochial, social scene and the Saudi mothers' aspirations to wealth, family and status for their daughters.

A shout startles me, and looking up I see Smiley on top of a ladder, his head hidden in clusters of dates. 'Spontaneity is the spice of life' I mutter to myself, dashing to my rooms for a plastic bag – talking to myself is becoming an alarming habit.

"Smiley – Phyllis pick dates, please?" I beckon him down and climb up the tall ladder exhilarated. What is it like to pick the fruit from one of the oldest plants in Arabia? The date palm has grown here for four thousand years. A palm needs less water than any other food crop, grows to thirty metres, and bears fruit for two centuries. A single tree yields up to one hundred kilos of dates. Highly nutritious, dates contain fifty four percent sugar and seven percent protein.

I stand in the branches; the power, the toughness, the strength of this ancient creation that endures the harshest of conditions and thrives. It seems to give out energy which I can absorb. It makes me feel better. I reach out to try to break off one of the long stems on which the dates grow. It is too tough. In my excitement I have forgotten Smiley uses a knife.

"Ma'am, come down. I get some – come." Smiley isn't smiling.

I am not in my garden picking apples! Date harvesting is a skill. I am shaky at the bottom of the ladder. I watch Smiley cut clusters of dates to be sorted and packed. Every part of the tree is used; poor quality dates and pits as animal fodder, leaves for roofs, mats and baskets. Smiley fills my plastic bag for me.

"This – good date Ma'am – best – name *khalas*." I agree the Palace dates are the most succulent.

Smiley wears a white cotton boiler suit and a white cotton *ghutra* on his head. He is a dark and handsome boy, and his long legs carry him speedily to the treetops. He asks me:

"I want – London Mrs Phyllis – I want London – I clean your house."

I am hungry. My lunch and late dinner usually ordered by Princess Abtah will not be served, I haven't been to the supermarket, it is 8.00pm, the cooks will be preparing an evening meal for the staff, no one speaks English. I dial the number Jo-Jo wrote down for me, rehearsing what to say.

"*Na'am*," a voice answers – yes.

"Er…er…*areed akl, shukran*" – I'd like food, thank you.

I recognise the word '*wayn*' – where?

"*Hunaa – hunaa shukran*" – here, here thank you – "Phyllis – *mudarissa Ingilizi.*" Phyllis, English Teacher I mutter pathetically.

The phone goes dead. Yes, the English are lazy about learning foreign languages.

An hour passes. The Hollywood movie channel is banned. Saudi programme planners have delved into the archives for family programmes extolling good moral values. Lassie trots confidently across my TV screen, interrupted by loud banging on my door.

When I open it the bearer has disappeared, leaving me a large tray carrying three foil-covered plates. I remove the foil. Oily spinach, greasy chicken and a sad salad with no dressing. I keep the salad and put the rest in the bin.

My eyes fall on my new toaster. That's what I need. Comfort food! Familiar food. Food that reminds me of home, hot crunchy toast and sweet scented honey and a pot of tea made with the good quality Assam tea leaves I found in a Riyadh supermarket.

Tomorrow I will find the staff kitchen. Tomorrow I will swim, do my Yoga.

Tonight in bed, I toss and turn, out of tune with my world.

I am a gregarious woman. I need someone to talk to outside the palace walls.

Chapter Fifteen
Making the Best of It

Trying very hard to be positive I think back to the list of people who were good to me when I was a newcomer and a little lost.

Amira's ladies who live with their husbands in bungalows on the periphery of the Palace, the office staff and the drivers and their children welcomed me. Soha, a Lebanese woman married to the Company Manager, especially. She had three daughters. When I met her she was carrying her fourth child and she and her family prayed for a son.

The eldest son is the second most important person in a Saudi family. A boy is born with great rejoicing and prayers of thanks to Allah. He has a privileged life, compared to his sisters.

When I needed a hairdresser, Soha gave me the address of the only reputable one in Hail. Ahmed was on holiday in Pakistan so *Amira* called Nasr, the Sudanese driver to take me. I didn't feel comfortable with Nasr. He laughed raucously at my attempts to speak Arabic, and only ever said 'Heello' and 'Bee-Bee' to me, in a loud, comic voice as if he were telling a joke. He had a habit of swinging his *subbah* – prayer beads – while he waited restlessly for a passenger. He was a swarthy menacing forty year old and I'd seen him lose his temper – definitely an unpredictable character, one to be wary of.

Nasr frowned as he toured the town looking for 'Salon Fatima.' Clutching the address in his hand, he didn't appear to know the street. He stopped twice to ask the way and muttered to himself irritably.

"*Hunaa, hunaa!*" – here, here! – he shouted. He wasn't in a good mood. I stepped out of the car by a rundown lock-up shop with no display sign and peered through the window. A woman was ironing a pile of clothes. It was a laundry – and Nasr was accelerating away!

"Nasr! Nasr!" He did not hear me...I ran down the narrow street in my long black *abaya* screaming at him to stop.

The car screeched to a halt, there was a better side to Nasr's nature. To get back to the Palace alone...how could I have...a woman alone in a street in Saudi Arabia is in a horrible plight... and I'd only just arrived.

I pressed the intercom of a more presentable shop front and a female voice answered: 'Fatima'.

"*Nasr – hunaa khamsa – shukaran.*" – Here – at five – thank you.

Nasr held up five fingers and nodded, "Bee-Bee!" In the Range Rover he shouted in his loud voice, "Seee-yooo!" I sincerely hoped I would.

Fatima was a dressmaker – hairdressing salons are always at the back of other shops – and I stepped into the clatter of sewing machines and the lively chatter of Filipino women.

"Hello – I help you?"

I asked for Fatima.

"No problem – come here." Brenda led me through into a small dull room with a grey linoleum floor and brown walls, a few faded hairdressing posters and two black plastic chairs. Fatima sat behind a large wooden desk by the only single-bar electric heater – January in Hail is cold.

I had been warned that dressmakers in Hail are notorious gossips. I tried to respond to Fatima's interrogations about Palace life with the necessary diplomacy and discretion. I needed to keep my job!

Brenda learnt hairdressing in her father's barber shop in Manila where she had a three year old daughter. Her husband disappeared so Brenda's mother looked after the child. She seemed afraid of Fatima, one of two wives who had started up her business with her dowry plus money from her husband. I felt anxious about Brenda, I'm not sure why.

Soha told me to bargain over the bill. A travel guide advised: '*a good bargainer establishes eye contact to appraise the opponent. Each looks into the other's eyes, searching for hints of strength and weakness.*' I looked searchingly into Fatima's calculating dark brown eyes, saying in what I though was a 'bargaining' voice: "How much?"

"240 SR," she replied – which is about forty pounds and twice what I pay my English hairdresser for better service. I started low: "130."

"200," came the reply. I opened my purse. I had brought 150 with me. I put it on her desk and showed her my empty purse. She accepted.

After a price is agreed the effort is traditionally rewarded with a gift symbolising a confirmation of friendship. Fatima presented me with a camel-skin waistcoat she had made by hand herself. I felt I had done pretty well, all things considered.

Soha's husband's position meant she always sat near to the Princess, and gave social gatherings for Princess Abtah in her bungalow. When I first arrived, Soha invited me to a party to celebrate *Eid*. I didn't feel like going, I had a terrible cough. I was not well and I had a sore ankle from jumping out of bed to answer a phone call I was expecting from my son – the operators soon stopped trying. I felt very sorry for myself.

Soha's bungalow was like an English pre-fabricated wartime building. The front door opened into a large room, with a dining room and a sitting room on either side, a kitchen and three bedrooms. There was a dining table and chairs, brightly-coloured sofa, armchairs, curtains and carpets and many ornaments and plastic flowers. All of the twelve staff bungalows are in the same style each with a small back garden. Princess Abtah gave permission for a grassy area to be a playground for the children and provided a roundabout and swings.

When Soha's invitation came I was at my lowest, and beginning to need a doctor, but I was a 'new girl' and I had been told that refusing invitations in royal circles is an insult.

I found a comfortable chair in the circle Arab ladies make.

"You – OK – you well?" A woman sitting next to me asked. I had been coughing rather a lot! I shook my head, I didn't feel like speaking.

"I doctor – name Bedour. I send medicine for cough – to Soha – ask Princess you go doctor." In her limited English, Bedour told me that she and her engineer husband were Syrians working in Saudi because they could earn much more money. I liked Bedour, and felt better. She gave me her phone number – a lifeline I badly needed then.

It was an effort to sit down on the carpet to eat. When the taped music and hand drums for dancing began I slipped quietly away. I was depressed and felt sorry for myself.

In my room I had a good cry. My foot hurt, I missed my husband, and I wanted to go home. My cough kept me awake in the night.

The next morning Princess Abtah gave me a letter: "This from Prince – for doctor - go Ahmed – hospital." I caught my breath. Hospital? I wasn't that bad! Bedour had said something about private patients going to the doctor at the hospital. I hoped she was right.

The waiting room was full; Ahmed spoke to a nurse and gave her the letter.

"Please," she beckoned to me to follow, taking me to a ladies' waiting-room. Mothers and babies, women of all ages, all with their faces covered, sat waiting. Ahmed stayed in the car. In no time at all, the nurse returned. Was I getting VIP treatment?

"Come – you Phyllis – Prince Muqrin Palace?" I nodded, full of apprehension. The doctor, an Egyptian, sat behind a desk.

"Hello, Mrs Phyllis – you sick?"

"Oh, no," I put on a smile, "only a cough." I wished I hadn't come.

The nurse helped me off with my blouse. I lay down on a couch. The doctor examined my throat and chest and returning to the desk he wrote out a prescription.

"Go with nurse." Confused, I followed her along a corridor to a small room with one bed in it. She wheeled a machine, with long pipes attached, up to the bed. She tilted the bed by a lever. The doctor came in.

"Lie down please – we clear chest with tube." My legs felt weak. I took a deep breath, getting a grip of myself. I waved my prescription.

"Medicine please – OK? No tube – medicine. Thank you."

I shook his hand and hurried out to find Ahmed and the dispensary.

That was the only time I needed a doctor in Saudi Arabia. I worked at keeping healthy, eating whole foods, rice, pasta, cereal, pulses, fruit, vegetables, with nothing added and nothing taken away, organic if possible, at least five pints of mineral water every day, and not much fruit juice, fresh air, exercise and yoga relaxation. Well, that was the ideal. It took a lot of effort to make it work in that culture and environment.

The climate dried out my skin and hair. Jo-Jo gave me some of her coconut oil, teaching me how to massage it into my hair, wrap in a hot towel and leave it for an hour before a shampoo.

In the *souk* in Hail I bought cheap almond body oil in a tiny shop selling exotic perfumes, oils and soap. Saudi men and women generously apply scent to their bodies, liberal splashes on their hands after washing. *Dehn-al-ward,* the essence of crushed rose petals, remains my favourite.

Perfume is produced in Taif and the wild roses grow in the Al Hadda mountains. Rose water is used as a subtle flavour in cooking and to enhance drinking water. Jasmine scent and musk are popular but the most precious is *oude*, wood of aloes burnt over charcoal.

To thank Soha I gave lessons to her eldest daughter, Louloua, and to Ma-ha, who loved to teach the ladies in the Government literacy schemes.

Now, on my own I prepared lessons for Bander and Jo-Jo and art projects for Sarah, and I wrote letters but I was desperate to get out of the Palace. Who else did I know in Hail? I searched my diary, and saw the name Howazeen. Howazeen? The young teacher I met when I gave the talk at the ladies' college.

It was a beautiful name for a beautiful woman with a mystical, exotic look who painted kohl onto her eyelids and around the eyes in the traditional Bedouin way. At only twenty-two she had already studied at the college for four years, got married and had three children, gained a diploma and been offered a teaching post for the next academic year.

"Hello, Howazeen, it's Phyllis, the governess at the Palace."

"Hi, how are you?" a friendly voice with an American accent. In her teens her family lived in Washington for two years. Learning that I was alone in the Palace, she sends her driver over to fetch me. I feel like a child going to my first party.

I ring the intercom in the fortress walls around Howazeen's large house in the centre of Hail.

"It's Phyllis"

The pace of life is slow. I wait. The enormous solid metal door slowly opens. An empty doorway. No one stands there!

"Welcome Phyllis."

Where is the voice coming from? It sounds like Howazeen. I cautiously step inside. Howazeen is behind the door! She speaks to her driver, who is standing behind me, from her hiding position. I am taken aback. Who is she hiding from? Then it dawns on me. Of course, her face isn't covered. Standing in her doorway she might be seen from the street.

Howazeen shares the house with her parents, in the traditional Saudi way. Her husband is an airline pilot. She had an arranged marriage, but she did see a photograph of him before their wedding day.

It is a pleasure to be in her company. Howazeen, a symbol of the new, modern Saudi woman, with a job and a priority, is bright and intelligent.

Her ambition is to become an English lecturer at the University in Jeddah. Howazeen's sister, Yasmin, a trendy fifteen year old in jeans and T-shirt who is going back to Washington to study, brings in mint tea, served with the sickly sweet pastries Saudi women love to eat. The girls play me American and English pop music, we talk about poetry. We look at and discuss *Jane Eyre*, Howazeen's favourite novel.

I have a lovely time and thank them from the bottom of my heart. Howazeen gives me a small papyrus print she bought on her honeymoon in Egypt and in exchange I give her a recent English language study book.

My solitary ten days pass. Bedour comes to call on me with her children, my first visitors at the Palace. It is exciting to be the hostess for once.

Ahmed takes me to the farm, and I stay in my bungalow,

hoping for inspiration. Walking by the olive trees ready for harvesting one early morning, it comes to me: I will start to write a book. I hurry back and get out my note book.

Chapter Sixteen
Go with the Flow

"We've been deployed to Jordan, can you get a few days off to see me?" Hearing my younger son Jason's voice on the telephone, out of the blue, fills me with emotion. I need him here now to embrace and to tell him how much I love him. I want desperately for us to share our thoughts about our loss. Besides, a trip to Jordan would make up for missing out on Beirut! Impulsively I ring Princess Abtah, who has returned the day before.

"Phyllis – you need special paper – you no go Lebanon – no special paper."

The office informs me the special paper is an *iqama*. Legally employed residents must carry this document which is supplied by their sponsors. It was requested when I arrived but I am still making do with a work permit stamp on my passport. I could leave the country travelling on my own but I can't return without my *iqama*.

Well, *insh'Allah*!

I put on my *abaya* to cross to the men's section of the Palace, to ask about flights to Amman. Palace life is back to normal. Women servants walk to and fro along the garden paths. October in Hail is a perfect climate for me: seventy degrees Fahrenheit and a fresh breeze. Women do not have to cover in the garden or in the women's section of the Palace, but when we pass through the Prince's gate into the men's section we must. I throw my veil over my face.

Coming towards me are two ladies, also covered. The breeze catches their black veils and billows out their flowing *abayas*. Their complete absence of identity gives me ideas of intrigue, mystery, and clandestine meetings!

I hadn't experienced meeting like this before, just two dark anonymous shapes on a deserted walkway. As we drew nearer I wonder who they are. Uncertainty makes me feel nervous and uneasy. I stop, searching their eyes. It is impossible to recognise them.

"Hi, it's Phyllis!" Pausing briefly, they reply in turn:

"I – Maha" and "Hello Phyllis, I Soha." They pass on immediately. Women must not stop to talk in the men's section of the Palace. I feel cold. What am I doing walking about like this? I must be mad! "How long can I go on?" I mutter to myself on my way towards the palatial office building. I am conscious of staring eyes following every step.

In Riyadh, Lamia's driver took me to an efficient women's bank. Female-run banks, she told me, were opening in the major cities but in the new women's bank in Hail no one spoke English, my Arabic wasn't good enough, the clerk looked at me as if I was about to rob the place and I walked out in a huff!

Segregation of the sexes in the workplace or anywhere is awful.

There are debates on women working in the English speaking newspapers, and restriction to the home is slowly being relaxed.

Women writers claim that women work in their own right, and not in competition with men. Many Saudi women do not work for the money but for intellectual satisfaction and personal fulfilment or to have more of a social life.

The law says a woman owner of a shop must employ male shop assistants but in Riyadh there is a multi-storied market built exclusively for women, with women shop assistants. It houses over two hundred shops for books, lingerie, ready-to-wear garments, *abayas*, jewellery and children's wear. It also has a restaurant and a play area for children and everything is owned and run by women.

No longer assuming the inferior role conferred on them by men, women run offices, schools, hospitals, banks, laboratories, Government social services, and are beginning to show media skills, especially on television and in journalism. Female entrepreneurs have the finance but they still lack personal freedom and they are not impressed by all western values.

Three weeks pass and no sign of my *iqama*. My son telephones me to say he is returning to the UK. I am down in the dumps again. On our way to pick up the girls from school, I tell Ahmed how fed up I am.

"You English lady – from Royal Family. Prince big responsible for Phyllis, no good travel alone." I am not consoled, I am deeply upset to think that my son has been so near.

"What kind of attitude is that?" I begin to feel angry. "I'm perfectly capable of looking after myself. I'm not a Muslim woman, I'm western, why do I have to conform?"

"Yes, Phyllis, Saudi difficult for ladies," Ahmed agrees and confides to me how he wishes he could take his wife and family back to Pakistan to live and work on the farm he owns with his brother.

"No like car all day – and women. Only women tell me what I do!" Ahmed was *Amira's* and Jowaher's driver. "I – boss in Pakistan – but money good here – Princess, good woman. I wait – save more – children better school in Pakistan – go later."

My driver is really the only person I can bare my soul to.

An English teacher I met at the Royal wedding in Jeddah told me she was so lonely that she ended up in the arms of her Sudanese driver! I resolve to sit always on the back seat of the Cadillac and to keep myself well covered. Ahmed and I...no!

"We go picnic." Princess Abtah sits in her day sitting-room, by her internal telephones and her mobile, busily arranging an outing for her friends, their daughters and the Palace ladies.

"Wear nice dress, ladies' picnic beautiful."

We drive in the usual convoy, for only a short distance to a public open space, a play area with swings, roundabout, climbing frame, an unkempt, apparently unused boating lake and a small fairground. Empty cans of coke, plastic bags, crisp packets, litter the scrubland.

Further off in the mountains' shadow, a large black Bedouin goatskin tent has been pitched. Ladies – old, middle-aged and young – teenagers and children arrive in expensive cars and People Carriers. Older Saudi ladies all with their heads and some with their faces covered, still wear ankle length straight skirts and hip length jackets, or long-sleeved simple dresses, their long hair tied back or in a bun.

But some of the teenage girls wear jeans, tight sweaters or T-shirts, trainers and western haircuts. At a party Jo-Jo gave at the Palace, one teenager turned up in a short skirt, a midriff top and high-heeled boots! Image is important to them and they are influenced by Spice Girl videos, fashion and the modern soap operas on television. However, a lot of girls seem to like the protection the *abaya* gives them.

The ritual coffee ceremony welcomes guests and large trucks arrive bearing enormous vats of food, delivered from a local restaurant. Platters are laid out on a big plastic tablecloth which covers most of the brightly-coloured carpet. The monotonous menu is brightened by dishes I haven't tried: *okra* – 'ladies fingers' served in tomato sauce, *saliq* – lamb cooked in spicy milk and rice flavoured with saffron, raisins and pinenuts. I am always put off by the *ghee*, an oily kind of butter that the food is cooked in: death to any diet!

After the three sittings – royal ladies and friends, young girls and children and finally the servants – the tent is cleared for dancing. Six women – completely covered in black – begin setting up microphones and warming their hand drums over the outside fire. Intrigued by this I ask Lamia, who was visiting her mother, what they were doing?

"It – hand drum – animal skin wrapped round wooden frame – to get er – sound – no," she thought for a moment.

"Pitch?"

"Yes, pitch – it warm over fire for this." Lamia says the musicians are young college students who formed their own band. The loud, raw, rhythmic sound I am used to starts but this group is different. Fresh, more zestful. I like the sound they make.

Practised in the skills of Saudi dancing I join in with the women in this ritual for self-expression. As always smiles and clapping welcome me. The atmosphere is convivial, the feelings warm and friendly, everybody is having fun. Even Muma Hasna sways to the music, on her stick. I find their obvious pleasure and mine, in sharing this freedom of the spirit, is always deeply moving.

Out of breath, I find a welcome seat next to a girl I met when she gave a party in her parents' ostentatious house in Hail. Her English is good and she has a brash, up front manner, not the usual Arab dignity. I remember her name is Hoda. An ornate gold comb grips her frizzy hair off her tough face. She holds a heart-shaped silver box from which she takes small squares of peppermint chewing gum.

"You like Palace – Hail?" she asks, her jaws moving rhythmically as she chews. Before I can answer, she goes on, "It's the pits – a dead dump." She offers me a can of coke. When I refuse she swigs it down herself. The music stops and as the dancers move to their seats, a large bottom knocks Hoda's coke from her hand.

"Oh, fuck!" she exclaims. Out of the corner of my eye I see her look at me under her thickly mascara'd eyelashes to check the effect. 'Fuck' is now such a universal English expletive it has lost its power to shock but I think it is my duty as an English governess first of all to ask her the true meaning of the word and if she doesn't know, to tell her. Second to explain that the word is socially taboo.

"It is as unacceptable as showing your face in a public place."

Hoda is silent for a moment and I wonder what she is thinking.

"Mmm…sorry…OK, thanks" is all she says.

In the chill night the women are gathered round the open fires, roasting chestnuts and drinking hot ginger tea. Lamia is talking to the musicians, and I go over to sit with them. I ask her to tell me why they haven't removed their *abayas* and face covering while they perform. In a conventional place like Hail it is not considered respectable for young women to play music and perform in public.

Lamia says the girls are self-taught, and manage and organise their performances themselves. I ask her to congratulate them on their music and the singer's voice. It is so much more professional and pleasing than the band I heard at the royal wedding in Jeddah.

"*Shukran*," I say, kissing the covered cheeks of the singer who is the leader of the band. The others giggle. The singer says something to Lamia.

"Aisha said you, funny – nice English lady, maybe you get for them recording contract?" Lamia translates. How I wish I could see their faces.

My weirdest experience of this anonymity is in an audience of women in an auditorium for a Health Education meeting. *Amira* is invited to present diplomas to newly qualified Saudi nurses. Nearly half of the women sit for the entire two and a half hours with their faces covered. The others wear their *abayas* and head covering.

A Saudi doctor gives a lecture advising women to use their National Health doctor, and not the traditional Bedouin women who prescribe natural cures. Next, slides instruct them on how long to boil goat, camel, sheep, or cow's milk to sterilise it for babies. There has been an outbreak of enteritis in Hail. The projector breaks down several times, and it is bizarre to witness the entire audience throwing their veils over their faces in unison when the male technician appears.

Chapter Seventeen

Aspects of Love

For over a year I have lived with women. I do think about men. As soon as I open my eyes in the morning, I think about John. If I cannot do up a necklace I miss him. If I hurt myself. If I think about the future. Or having morning tea together – we both loved that time.

If I had gone to Saudi Arabia and I could not get home, he would have been my white knight and come to rescue me. He would have done so – I know. I missed him taking me to the airport when I left, and I will miss him meeting me when I return.

He was my only confidant, my best friend. I could tell all my troubles to him, and be totally myself. I met him when I was seventeen, so I knew him all my adult life. He was the anchor between me and our children. He was always there when I needed him, losing him is lonely and so hard to bear.

It is a surprise when I even notice a man, especially as I hardly ever see one.

His Royal Highness Prince Muqrin has his own Palace door. In his separate part of the Palace he carries on a formal life and welcomes guests. When he finishes work in the afternoon and comes home for a siesta, and at night, he enters the royal apartments.

I see him on the oyster marble staircase sometimes, when I am going up in the early evening to prepare lessons in the study room, and the Prince is on his way down. He has perfect manners. He will always say: "Good evening, Phyllis – how are you?" Once, soon after a Royal wedding, he asks me if I enjoyed myself at the celebrations.

I reply that it was very kind of Princess Abtah to invite me. She had no need. The Prince remarks it is a very different wedding ceremony to an English wedding. I say it is an unforgettable experience. His manner is gracious, and I have observed his love for Princess Abtah – the way he looks at her and hurries to her apartments. Now on the marble staircase I get a fluttery feeling. He is a handsome man in his hand-woven, gold braided, camel-hair flowing cape.

In the royal house in Jeddah on another day, again the Prince is leaving. His limousine waits to take him to a function with King Fahd. I also am going out into the courtyard. I am astonished when he opens the big door for me. "Please, Phyllis," he says, and I walk through ahead of him.

All Arab men believe all western women have loose morals. Just as western women believe all Arab men have voracious sexual appetites. The Prince has Omar Sharif eyes, and a pleasing approachable manner.

Meeting him alone on the marble staircase, and again in the Jeddah house, are the only two occasions I am alone with him, and each time I feel his sensuality. The sensation stays with me for days.

One very hot afternoon I encounter Professor Mohammed. Princess Abtah is away from the Palace, and I take a risk and wear a sun-dress which I know I should not do. I am hoping no one is about. My arms are bare and my legs are bare from just below the knee and I am heading for a secluded part of the gardens.

I come out of my rooms and walk towards the huge outer door. Professor Mohammed's study door opens, and he stands there in front of me. Our eyes meet. He stands quite still. I can feel a rush in my breathing. My hair is blonde and he has probably never seen a blonde woman. He knows he should not be alone with me. It is a jailable offence.

The look in his eyes burns my skin. He is lost for a moment. I can feel a chemistry begin to work between us. He looks away and walks quickly through a different study room door.

The hallway, where the teachers take Arabic coffee or mint tea breaks, is painted a hideous bright red – even the ceiling. Three buttercup yellow sofas dazzle against the red walls.

Passing along this hallway to the garden on another afternoon, I see Professor Mohammed in his full-length white cotton *thobe* and red checked *ghutrah*, taking his break with a colleague. Ali, a servant, says to me, "Phyllis – you like coffee?"

I say, "No thank you – I prefer mint tea." The cardamom in Arabian coffee always makes me feel queasy.

Ali fetches mint tea, and the Professor asks me if the children are good students.

I tell him that their Arabic lessons take up so much time, there's not enough for me, and I'd like their timetable altered.

He says that Bander has to pass his Arabic college exams, and Jo-Jo her high school exams.

I do not want to upset him, and I know I must respect his status in the Royal household hierarchy, or I will make him lose face. If I go on with this conversation, he has no alternative but to tell me he can do nothing about it, and I have to speak to Prince Muqrin. Anyway, I doubt I can change anything. The rhythm of life here has been the same for so long.

"I like – speak English," the Professor says, so I tell him about when I visited a Bedouin family and the elder Bedouin gave me a *rebabah*.

We are standing. I am wearing the loose long-sleeved Arabic dress, the *jellabia*. My head is uncovered. He is looking at me. It is unusual for him to talk to me. He is permitted only because a colleague and the servants are present.

Arab men make no gestures nor do they show any expression on their faces. The Professor says: "I play – *rebabah*."

I am amazed because it is a Bedouin instrument. The Professor is a Saudi, so his ancestors were Bedouins. His grandfather, or his father, must have taught him.

"Would you play it for me?" I am so impressed that I turn and race back to my room, thinking 'he won't stay…he'll be gone when I get back.'

I am running, and I am really excited when I see the hallway again – and he is still there.

"Here it is, Professor."

Out of breath, I hand him the instrument.

He sits down on the yellow sofa and puts the *rebabah* between his legs, in the folds of his white *thobe*, as if it is a cello.

He lifts the bow. He begins to play.

A *rebabah* is a simple cello with horsehair strings and a horsehair bow. The sound is raw and primitive.

I am bewitched – it is a poetic moment that I will always remember. He plays in quite a faltering way, but I find him unbelievably sexual...he just attracts me...I think it must be the mystery of the unknown...I shall never love an Arab man...but I stand there imagining what a love affair would be like.

I think he suddenly realises what he is doing – he stands up suddenly, hands the instrument to me, acknowledges me with a brief bow of his head, and moves quickly to the door, his colleague following. He leaves without saying goodbye.

Professor Mohammed has disturbed me. He has not only awakened my romantic nature, he has challenged my status as a governess. It is necessary for me to make a stand about my lesson times and the haphazard attendance of my Royal pupils. I catch Princess Abtah in her day sitting-room after school the next day.

"You – always strict – serious – for lessons, Phyllis – I like." *Amira* is on my side.

"I would like Bander and Jo-Jo's mobile number so as to contact them when they are late for my lessons." Starting lessons on time is a discipline they need to be aware of and I have a 'bee in my bonnet' about punctuality.

"If Jowaher or Bander miss lessons, they must apologise."

The princess looks blank.

"Say sorry," I repeat.

"No Bander – no Jowaher – ring me – I find," she says.

Teaching English as a foreign language allows the teacher to be creative and imaginative, which suits me. In Greece, Italy and Spain I liked teaching with lots of interaction.

At my gilt-edged, marble-topped desk in the light, airy study room I review my situation. This job is certainly not as pressurised or demanding as state school teaching at home. My students respect me. I don't have staff meetings or homework to mark, and I am my own boss, at least for my teaching programme.

If only I can organise more time for them to study with me, I have the energy and enthusiasm to teach them. It is frustrating that they could learn so much more. I know I am not challenged. I was an actress. I can direct plays, teach drama, dance and Yoga. Then I remind myself that, like all expats and migrant workers, I came here because I needed money.

At the next lesson, they are on time, both chewing gum. I noticed *Amira* and some of the ladies chewing gum the previous evening. "It's bad manners to chew gum in the classroom ," I say in my headmistress voice. Jo-Jo does as she is told, Bander, always up to tricks, opens his mouth:

"Look – it's gone – I've swallowed it!" I know it is stuck to the roof of his mouth. A seventeen year old Arabian Prince isn't going to take an English governess that seriously – but even so, I continue undaunted.

"Can we have English conversation?" It is the easiest choice and Bander does look tired. It is 7.30pm and he says they have come from Arabic lessons without a break – though they have slept for two or three hours after lunch.

All foreign students find English grammar difficult, especially the perfect tense and phrasal verbs that are a nightmare! Bander and Jo-Jo are no exception. As a treat I finish the lesson with a 'gap fill' exercise. I play a Beatles song that I think will be relevant to their lives: *Can't buy me love*.

Their listening skills are very good, and after playing the tape a couple of times they quickly fill in the missing words. When we have finished correcting intonation and pronunciation, we sing the song together.

"Play it again – again!" Bander is very enthused by the energetic, infectious rhythm.

"Let's dance!" Jo-Jo throws herself about. Bander lifts up his *thobe* and chucks off his *ghutrah*, gyrating and shaking to the music. The study room rocks! They sing at the tops of their voices.

"Ye-eah…money can't buy me love…money can't buy me love."

I say I hope the meaning of the song will come true for them. I'm sure it gave them something to remember. Strangely enough, neither of them had ever heard of the Beatles.

Sarah never comes voluntarily to my study room, her nanny brings her, or I collect her.

"I busy – study Arabic lessons – I pray." Her usual tactic is to tear off as fast as she can with me in hot pursuit, along the Palace corridors, round the corners, to the study room where she rushes in and hides. That's her favourite ploy, and "can we do art?" She loves drawing and painting, but most days it's just to get her out of studying.

"When you've done your spelling test and used your dictionary," I respond firmly. I have noticed in a written test from her school that many English words she knows and can pronounce she spells incorrectly. She has never used a dictionary before I came to the Palace and she seems to enjoy looking up words in a small handy one published for young foreign students. Emulating her brother and sister makes her feel grown up.

Sarah does some good art work. The best, for me, is her painting of the Hale-Bopp comet. I have the privilege of seeing Hale-Bopp through the lens of a telescope in Prince Muqrin's Observatory, built for him on his farm. The Prince's assistant, Rudi, a young Indian son of the office manager, says Prince Muqrin is a keen astronomer, giving hospitality to fellow astronomers from abroad.

The first time I am aware of the comet will remain vivid in my memory. I enter my study room to prepare lessons. It is a lovely night, so I open my large French windows on to the balcony. The long, floaty, white drapes that cover the windows catch the breeze as the doors open covering my face, then, as I step blindly outside I hear a voice:

"Good evening, Phyllis." My heart leaps up into my throat! Pulling the drapes from my face, I see Prince Muqrin. He is not alone; his suave Indian personal aide Charles is with him, setting up a large camera on the balcony.

"Look – can you see the Hale-Bopp comet?" He moves near to me, gesturing out towards the stars. "It has a very bright head and a long tail...can you see it?" I look, only conscious of his presence next to me.

"It's a beautiful night," I say, looking at him. Prince Muqrin has a compelling personality, and unquestionable sex appeal. His lustrous, dark, unfathomable eyes turn and hold mine: I am suspended in time and space. For one fleeting moment – I am in love!

"Phyllis…what you do?" Princess Abtah's ear is always near to the ground. She steps out on to the balcony, looking elegant as usual ready for the evening with her ladies in the *diwaniyah*. The spell is broken, and my feet touch the ground again. I return to my desk and get on with my work.

I talk briefly to Sarah about colours, texture and the effect she wants to create, and give her a gentle and occasional guiding hand and she produces a painting which is remarkable for one so young.

I would have liked to bring Sarah's painting of that comet back to England as a keepsake.

That evening, when we look at the painting again to check if it is dry, I say impulsively:

"Go and show it to your father…" Vincent Van Gogh once said, '*the only thing that matters is the force of one's expression*'.

She returns with a zestful exhilaration that only the very young possess and hands me her painting. At the bottom, written in English in stylish handwriting, are the words: 'You are my star. I love you. Daddy.'

Chapter Eighteen

Hail

Gabby tells me she once drove from Riyadh to Hail disguised as a man and the thought has crossed my mind - gender could easily be disguised under all the flowing garments and headgear. Apparently a man was once arrested at a Royal wedding wearing an *abaya* and a veil. He was sitting in the entrance to the hotel by where the women left their *abayas* - he was spotted because of his large feet, grubby socks and flip-flops.

I photograph the mud-brick Rashid Palace that still stands in Hail with its palm log beams, and I see the decorated mosque inside the Palace near the Governor's building, where Prince Muqrin works every day. As I snap away with my camera it seems to me that everyone stops what they are doing to stare at me. Men come out of their shops, passers by halt in their tracks. Ahmed calls to me:

"They not see – lady take picture. Phyllis, get in car – we not want – problem!"

I like Hail and the province of the same name. The changing climate suits me and the clear air is heavenly. As I drive out of the Palace gate into the desert scrub, past goat and sheep herds, the remote tranquillity gives it a biblical feel. In the town, cars and trucks zoom through the narrow, dusty streets, shattering the silence. Tourists are rarely seen, there are no hotels and only one supermarket. *Amira* shops in Jeddah.

McDonald's and Pizza Hut have arrived just before me. Run-down lock-up shops line the streets selling cheap clothes, shoes, *thobes* and *abayas*, household goods, rugs and pottery. The gold *souk* and the fruit and vegetable market do a good trade. In the morning the smell of baking bread and perfume wafting from Saudi male passers-by on their way to work mingle with the heat and dust.

Shops and businesses are owned by Saudis, employees are immigrant workers where children work as child labourers from the age of nine. I see them carrying bundles and packages through the streets on my brief visits. The photographic shop is efficient and a general store selling stationery and school equipment has the basics I need.

Even in the cooler part of the day I soon need to quench my thirst. The small, primitive cafés are for men only. I usually buy a small bottle of water in a confectioner's shop and the only place to rest one's legs in the heat is on the doorstep. As soon as all the shops close for prayer, the women sit on the curb side to wait for their male drivers.

Once I open the door to a shop selling CDs and music tapes after I'd seen a Lebanese singer on the television and loved her voice and wanted to buy a tape of her songs. Ahmed hoots the horn of the car loudly and I turn to see him calling me over:

"Ladies not allowed in music shop."

I look at him in disbelief. "I want to choose my tape *myself*, I don't want a man to do it for me!" Western rage shows on my face, "Why…why…*why*?" I explode to Ahmed.

He shrugs his shoulders. "Listen music…get sexy. Phyllis make love on floor with man."

Remarks like that are best ignored, and besides, chance would be a fine thing!

Afterwards, Ahmed stops the car to buy *shawarma*, a Lebanese snack for his family. Layers of lamb or chicken are placed on the *shawarma* gas machine which slowly rotates to cook the meat that is then carved and served in pitta bread with sesame sauce – very tasty. Vegetarian *shawarma* is made with aubergines and courgettes. Ahmed knows I prefer this.

"Here Phyllis – this fed you up!"

"Cheer me up," I correct automatically. Foreigners can never get their heads round phrasal verbs.

In one month I will have been in my present employment for one year. The harmonious family feel of Palace life is agreeable, by now I know almost everybody in the Palace and everybody knows me. I have adapted as best I can to Saudi ways and customs, even the somewhat strange: never sit with your legs outstretched showing the soles of your feet; don't beckon with your index finger; laughter should be moderated, never raucous.

The discipline of working on my book helps put my life into perspective. I compile notes and I hide them in a safe and secret place – always suspicious that hidden eyes are watching me. I am already aware that my phone calls are monitored.

I have a rapport now with the teachers at Jo-Jo's and Sarah's school, and talk to Hala, the Egyptian teacher. The girls are good students, though Sarah is lazy and Jo-Jo, intelligent and able, is easily distracted in class. Their poor attendance record is due to trips to the farm, or to Riyadh or Jeddah.

Hala says: "Phyllis, we all speak about the beautiful English play – nobody in Hail see like that before – can we do again?"

I answer I will think about it. The prospect of all that effort, and the limits on what I can and can't do, fill me with trepidation. The lacklustre nature of Saudi female education dampens my spirits. The education standard is so low they need more creativity, imagination, colour and they also need updated text books and teacher training exchange schemes with the West.

Hala wants to return to Cairo, where she had a job as a translator for Cairo radio. "I feel like a prisoner here – I cry to see my parents, sisters and brothers – my husband want to stay because – good money."

"Well it's not forever," I reply optimistically, thinking it is not for me either.

The infant classes finish earlier and the younger children wait for their sisters and drivers. Before the upper school bell rings we stand together in the shade by the old wooden school door. Little girls, in their ankle-length navy blue pinafore dresses over long-sleeved white blouses, holding hands for support, cautiously come up to me saying playfully: "Hel-lo – how – har you – how – har you?" and then run away with squeals of delight as soon as I answer "Hello" and chase after them.

As time goes by more small children join in this game so I end up teaching them all to play *what's the time...mr wolf...?* – great fun, but for me, hiding my eyes and then whizzing round to run after the children, in this climate in my Arab clothes, is exhausting!

Back at the Palace, I pick up the receiver of the internal telephone and dial security. "Please open the swimming pool for English teacher…thank you." The Filipinos who man security all speak pidgin English.

In the gardens I see Princess Abtah at the huge bronze entrance door to the pool. Workers are carrying in long planks of wood.

"Can I swim?" I ask, wondering what is going on.

"Don't ask," is her reply – a well-known dismissive phrase used when she has a lot on her mind. I turn tail and walk away. The pool is temporarily drained and covered with planks, floor-covering and carpet, to make an extra banqueting hall for the visit of the Governor of Madinah and his wife. I will have to sacrifice one of my few daily pleasures.

A frenzy of activity begins. Silver tableware, platters, fruit bowls, *dallahs* – coffee pots – and tea pots are cleaned and polished. *Amira's* sitting room is buzzing. I see her with Lamia making lists and telephoning orders.

On the day, the Governor and his wife arrive in style at the Prince's gate with a police escort. There they part company, he to Prince Muqrin's reception room, his wife to *Amira's*. Visitors congregate from far and wide, relatives stay in luxury apartments in various palatial buildings.

'What can I wear this evening?' It is the third and final day of the celebrations. Choosing a dress for special occasions is always a problem. I don't possess many clothes appropriate for Saudi society and I seem to have ended up with three suitable outfits, ringing the changes as one would a uniform.

I take out a dress I haven't worn lately and stepping into it, I begin to zip up the back. To my dismay, I can't get the zip over my thighs and bottom. I rush to the mirror – my stomach bulges as well! I have put on weight! I know I have been over-indulgent with the food for the past couple of days.

Two Lebanese chefs who have trained in French cuisine and own a restaurant in Jeddah are flown to Hail especially, so the food is of a different quality. Real French delicacies, crunchy not soggy vegetables, salads with French dressing – never seen in Saudi Arabia, meats not overcooked and fresh, not frozen fish – and hot baked French bread!

The meals aren't served in courses, you just sit down on a gilt chair at a long marble table set out with spoons and forks, and small individual bottles of Coca-Cola and water, and help yourself. Servants stand round in a laid-back fashion. After the first meal I go to the kitchen to compliment the young chefs. Their tall white hats shake with laughter as I describe my battles with sheep's eyes, stomach and sticky feet.

No wonder I am growing plump, there have been a spate of 'food gatherings'. The ladies from the Palace were invited to the farm to cook their own favourite meal Bedouin style - with pots simmering on open fires, Maha prepared a birthday party for Jowaher and a teacher from Jo-Jo's school invited me for a typical Egyptian meal at her house.

I do believe in the saying 'you are what you eat,' but I am human and stress slows down the metabolism causing the body to put on weight. Psychological well-being is the key to good health.

Maybe John's death and the effort I put into this complete change of lifestyle are taking their toll.

In my room I turn round slowly, looking ruefully at my body from all angles in the mirror panels. I have put on a good few pounds – I will ask *Amira* if I can weigh myself on the scales in one of her bathrooms. I make a stern resolve to go on a diet, and change into a looser-fitting dress, clip on my long, delicate, hand-made gold earrings – the spoils of bargaining in the *souk* – and brace myself for the gourmet feast ahead!

Confident of the formal arrival procedures, I walk into the banqueting hall to greet Princess Abtah and her guests. She is seated at the head of the customary large circle of comfortable sofas and big armchairs. Flowers glow under the chandelier-lit hall, and little gilt-edged, glass-topped tables are scattered about, bearing dates, nuts and chocolates. The oyster marble swimming hall has been transformed.

I take the limp hand of the Governor's wife, I don't remember her name. "*As salaam alaikum*" I said, "*Wa alaikum as salaam*" she replies. She is over-dressed in pink and light mauve. Her cheeks are heavily rouged, her lips painted dark red. On top of her head her unnaturally dyed red hair has been wound round in a pile. Jewels flash everywhere. As she stands up to greet me, it crosses my mind that she looks like a faded movie star from the early Hollywood days.

I continue my protocol rounds, kissing women I know on both cheeks and shaking the hand of strangers. The room is enormous. I kiss about fifty women, it's exhausting. I sit down to rest next to a woman I have never met but Arab women do not remain strangers for long. Leila is the daughter of Prince Muqrin and his first wife, whom he divorced a few years after he married Princess Abtah. She looks in her late thirties, confident and capable. She has a brother and two sisters and lives with her two sons in Jeddah, divorced from her husband. I said how surprised I am to meet a divorced woman in Saudi Arabia and she agrees it is unusual, Islam is against divorce and encourages spouses to do their utmost to keep marriage strong and harmonious. How difficult it must be for a divorced Muslim woman to live alone, even when she is as privileged and wealthy as Leila.

To be divorced the *qu'adi* – judge, appoints an arbiter for each family to find out the facts, but their objective must be reconciliation. The *Qur'an* states '*Of all things licit, the most hateful is divorce*' and '*if you wish to have a wife in place of a divorced one, do not return her dowry, even if it be a talent of gold. That would be improper and grossly unjust, for how can you return when you have lain with each other and entered into a firm contract.*'

The *Qu'ran* exhorts a separated man to be 'considerate and kind' to his former wife, to maintain and support her and not eject her from their house. If the judge decides reconciliation has failed a formal document is eventually issued.

Muslim women are hardly ever allowed to exercise their right to divorce. Tremendous social and mental pressures subject them to barriers they need enormous courage to cross, which most of them lack, so divorce in Islam has effectively become an exclusive right of men.

In the banqueting hall the crowd of women ranges from the elderly to teenagers. Friends from Hail, their daughters, teachers from the school and the Ladies' College, and ladies of the Palace mix with extravagantly dressed Arabian princesses. Uniformed servants – dressed in dark green ankle length skirts and long jackets, their heads covered in small gold braided gauze scarves – who have been flown in from an agency in Riyadh, parade round serving coffee, mint tea, chocolates and dates.

We finish dinner and I feel full but very contented. The food is delicious - my attempt to stick to salads has failed. The band has been pulsating away, a well-known female singer moves through the crowd singing Middle-Eastern pop songs that everybody knows. Dancing begins and I join in hoping to dance away any bulges!

Some visiting princesses bring their own beauticians and hairdressers and one Egyptian hairdresser is an expert belly dancer. The atmosphere livens up and inhibitions are released. The hairdresser is pulled into the middle of the hall to clapping and encouraging calls. Slim, with a beautiful figure, her long dark tresses below her bottom, she throws off a jacket, reveals a bare midriff and begins to dance.

Her natural alluring grace and her movements put western imitations utterly to shame. Witnessing her charm and talents I perhaps have a glimpse of what Salome's dance might have been like.

The performance enthuses other ladies to join the dancing and the floor is crowded. *Zaghareet* begins and its wild high-pitched vibrations bring Princess Abtah, who *never* dances, to join us. Her ecstatic friends make a close circle around the Princess, swaying with her, in joyful harmony.

Princess Abtah is related to the Rashid family, rivals of the Saud family, and Hail was once the capital of the Rashid who controlled the land north to Al Jawf, until King Abdul Aziz unified the country. Local people are proud she has married into the Saud family, but as a Rashid she is revered and loved by all.

The ladies will stay up until *Salat-al-fajr*, the prayer between first light of day and sunrise. Arab women have amazing stamina. One o'clock in the morning is late enough for me. As I am leaving, *Amira* calls me over. She looks amused, and Soha and Faiza sitting with her are also smiling.

"You like Saudi lady Phyllis - you get big bottom," she says for all to hear.

I am *not* amused!

Chapter Nineteen
Relationships

Human warmth is precious. There is a good feeling amongst these Muslim women, I am amongst a genuine sisterhood. I cannot speak their language but I observe and communicate by instinct, intuition, actions, expressions, sight, touch and mime.

Arabic seems a rich, expressive language, but too difficult for me to learn. Can I really say I know these women? Their thoughts, attitudes, beliefs, their bitchiness, jealousies, generosity and compassion? I can never quite reach them, their deep thoughts and feelings, maybe they would never allow any westerner to. Yet despite the handicaps I am sustained by real friendships, in my isolation.

Bedour, the Syrian doctor, has been a constant friend for a year now. I always telephone her - incoming calls for me are hit or miss, the Palace telephone switchboard has an unpredictable nature.

Hisham, her husband and their two children come and pick me up on a weekend for a meal at their house.

Thankfully Soha is near to sort out delays at Security and secure me a safe passage out of the Palace.

I have to be so careful on Hisham's account too. In a so-called local park with swings and a roundabout, I settle down on the scrub for a picnic lunch and remove my veil, to get some fresh air and enjoy a sandwich, before I notice an anxious look on his face:

"Please, Phyllis – cover – we not want trouble." We are near a desert road, cars and trucks zoom along at top speed. The *muttawa* patrol car could pass us at any time. Hisham and Bedour's jobs mean a lot to them. Deportation is on his mind.

The shabbiness of my surroundings beyond the gates – the boring urban scrub, the constant sound of the traffic, make me long for the well-ordered, designed and maintained public parks at home; the lush grass, trees and fields, the quiet colours of the rolling hills and valleys and I realise I am privileged and better off inside the walled freedom of the exquisite Palace garden.

My consolation is being in the company of Bedour and her family. The fun we have together; exchanging thoughts and ideas, singing English songs I teach the children, playing games and sharing a meal. I hope Bedour will come with Hisham and the children to visit me at home, their first visit to Britain.

I love Faiza too, she is an extremely attractive lively woman. She never wears the same dress twice when visiting the Palace.

"Lovely to meet you, darling!" are her first words to me, which bonds us from the start. Faiza, a Saudi diplomat's daughter lived and went to school in England. She married at sixteen and set off to Washington with her student husband. When the marriage didn't work out, she came here to study English at Jeddah University and married a wealthy Saudi businessman. Faiza has a busy life, four children and a demanding husband for whom she organises business dinners and events – never attending any, of course.

One evening, after a meal of deliciously different Middle Eastern dishes she cooks especially for me, she confides her longing to use her abilities in more fulfilling ways. She suffers from tension, headaches, stomach pains and feelings of anxiety – she has a stressful life. I know Yoga will help her, and she comes to my rooms the next day.

I call disharmony within a person 'dis-ease.' Yoga breathing creates harmony, a union of mind, body and spirit. It is twenty-five years ago now since I became 'hooked' on Yoga, practising daily, finding when I missed a session I wasn't so relaxed and flexible both physically and emotionally. I like the uncompetitive element, and how Yoga is very 'personal' and leads to self-realisation. The daily practice of Yoga and meditation are more important to me than words can say, and help me to survive in Saudi Arabia, and to calm the sorrow of losing John.

Faiza learns a short routine for her daily life, a way of helping her healing process. I give her a Yoga and relaxation tape I made and we practise Yogic breathing and *pranayama* – breath control – together, the key to unwinding and letting go. I am happily observing Faiza gradually benefiting from my lesson when the *asr* prayer call from the Palace mosque interrupts us. As I sit in meditation, encompassing universal energies, Faiza performs her afternoon prayers towards Makkah – an enthralling experience of mixed western, Asian and Islamic cultures.

It seems a western woman's friendship with a Saudi woman

can grow. A Saudi man is reluctant to speak with or look at a western woman, who in turn will keep her distance, and avoid eye contact. By contrast Arab men show their affection to one another freely in public. A greeting is a hug and a kiss on both cheeks, and in the shopping malls in Riyadh and Jeddah I often see young Arab men walking hand in hand, a sign of friendship which is in no way considered as sexually deviant behaviour.

Arab men seem to be open and loving as fathers and husbands. At the Palace the children will spend some time with Prince Muqrin every evening. He seems extremely interested in them and their academic progress, frequently asking to see their work, especially test results.

He and Bander are great companions, and often take their falcons hunting in the desert – his hooded falcons sit waiting patiently in a shaded spot in the Palace garden. One frosty January morning as Ahmed starts the Cadillac to drive us to school, Sarah spots Bander in his Range Rover:

"Hoot Bander – hoot Bander – he go hunting – drive fast, Ahmed!"

Bander's driver sees us in his mirror and pulls up. Jo-Jo and Sarah leap out to hug and kiss Bander goodbye as if they are never going to see him again.

He is going with his father and friends for a week. I compliment him on his coat.

"It's a *farwa*, the desert – very cold!"

A *farwa* is a Bedouin single sheepskin coat. Bander's modern version is long-sleeved and lined with several sheepskins.

Prince Muqrin and Princess Abtah are grandparents, and seem very much in love. They are never out of each other's company at

161

weekends, relaxing on the farm they have a deep compatible regard and affection for each other. I see them walking together hand in hand in the cool evenings inspecting Prince Muqrin's vegetable garden.

One foggy February weekend on the farm, Prince Muqrin, once a Major in the Saudi Airforce, is away, due to fly back in his own private plane to Hail airport. At lunchtime, the fog has closed the airport. As is the custom, after lunch we settle down in the big modern open plan sitting-room to watch TV, read, or play cards. Princess Abtah cannot settle, she paces around. She stops and gazes out of a window. By *maghrib* prayer, the fog is lifting slowly. After darkness has fallen, Security ring *Amira* from the entrance gate; Prince Muqrin has arrived. Relief and joy show for all to see on her face. She continues to stand, watching the huge glass-panelled entrance doors.

In a finely woven *bisht*, - black wool cloak, Prince Muqrin walks in at an eager pace, his eyes for one woman only. In a moment they are in each other's arms in a passionate embrace, which takes them, still embracing, slowly away to their private rooms.

Wandering away on my own in the darkness, along the dusty desert track to my bungalow, I think how lucky I am, that I too have known such a love myself, with my husband John. I have known the continuity, affection, and sense of belonging, that only the one you truly love can bring.

The final lyrics of a song Governess Anna sang in *The King and I* comes into my mind, and I sing as I walk:

All of my wishes go with you tonight
I've had a love like you.
I've had a love of my own like yours,

I've had a love of my own...

Anna was a widow and she too worked for a Royal Family to help her out of the financial difficulties she was left with. Thinking of her I feel less alone.

Chapter Twenty
The Young Ones

I am intrigued to see from my window a group of small boys walking through the garden looking neat and tidy in their *thobes* and *taqiyah* – the white skull cap that keeps the hair in place. Young boys wear the checked *ghutrah*, the *igaal* – a black braided cord doubled over and set on top of the *ghutrah*, is worn when they are older.

Who are they? Where do they live? Where are they going? I grab my camera, hurry out of my rooms and follow them at a distance, up to the garden gate leading to the men's quarters, there I remember to stop! I wait around, and take photographs of the Palace and the spectacular approach, the glorious garden and mountain backdrop.

I hear the prayer call at the mosque, where they must have gone, and I sit on a garden bench. Time passes pleasantly. The laughter and chatter of children breaks my contemplation: the boys. Standing up, I back away looking through my camera lens. They stop and pose instinctively, the shutter clicks, and they are immortalised for my scrap book.

They learn my name and I try to pronounce and remember theirs. From that day, I meet them regularly in their playground, where I love to spend time on a swing, soaring high above the Palace walls seeing views of the desert beyond; I watch them play football on a grassed area in the Palace gardens and visit their mothers in their bungalows.

Whenever and wherever I meet them, they always like to show off the little English they know.

"Hah-looo....hah aa yoo?" or "Pheelees...Hah-looo." In return for English phrases, they teach me simple Arabic phrases. Their giggly voices, the amused looks they exchange, bring me to the conclusion that to them I am completely eccentric, if not actually mad. But I like to think that individual eccentricity of the English is creative!

I do have a soft spot for Jowaher. She has a good strong sense of commitment but her privileged position distracts her very easily from her English studies. When she is late for her lesson I wander along the corridor to her rooms to find her huddled over school homework or her private lessons' work from Professor Muhammed. Learning the *Qur'an* and Arabic grammar, which she says is very difficult, takes up a lot of her time.

It is nearly the end of term, the *Ramadan* break is soon, and she is swotting for her final test. I sit down next to her on the sofa.

"How's it going?" She doesn't look up.

"I - nearly finish - I come - soon." I put my arm round her, and kiss her cheek. She looks paler than usual. Saudi girls get virtually no exercise and live constantly in air conditioning which I am sure depletes their energy levels. I can't be angry with her for being late.

Bander on the other hand is as elusive as the Scarlet Pimpernel. It is nearly the end of his exams and after lessons with Professor Muhammed he is off with his friends into Hail to Pizza Hut or McDonald's.

Jo-Jo lolls her head onto my shoulder and closes her eyes.

"I ha-a-ate to st-u-dy," she yawns the words sleepily. We sit for a while, appreciating the joys and precious quality of silence when obligations are forgotten.

"Jo-Jo – eat. She hungry – she tired," Lynda, Jowaher's personal servant – a tough, sturdy, Filipino woman of about thirty, who speaks her mind – plonks a tray on the table in front of us emphatically. I look at my watch, nine o'clock, the late evening meal for the Princesses and the daughters of Princess Abtah's ladies of the Palace is being served.

I get up, walk to the kitchen diner, select two slices of watermelon, over-cooked spaghetti with tomato sauce and a ruined soggy, too sweet *tiramisu* covered in artificial cream, and put them on a tray and return to Jo-Jo's room. We can practise English conversation over a meal as she won't be joining the others.

A year has gone full circle, and *Ramadan* is here again. It is December – cold mornings and chilly nights. I make my way along a corridor to the servants quarters near the *diwaniyah*. I often use Rahma's and Nafisa's spin dryer. They are lucky enough to have their own washing machine. No one answers my light taps on the door.

"Rahma…Nafisa…" I call, knocking louder, "It's Phyllis…" No answer.

A few steps away is their communal sitting room, where the servants sit waiting to be called, brew coffee and tea, chat and watch TV. Not a sign of anyone. Going back the way I came the *maghrib* prayer calls ring out from the Palace mosque.

Passing a reception room opposite to the *diwaniyah*, I notice sandals and shoes left outside the door, which is slightly ajar. Moving closer I hear a male voice chanting in prayer. I peep through the gap in the door. All I can see is a screen, the man is hidden from my view. Burning with curiosity, I open the door a little further. Opposite him a little distance away is a line of women, each one completely swathed in the light cotton cloth for prayer. For a moment I stand transfixed by the turquoise, cerise, jade green and silvery blue garments, and the rhythmic beauty of their prayers. Then, feeling guilty about my presence at this solemn occasion, I slip quietly away.

The *Imam* from the Palace mosque comes personally during *Ramadan*, to take the *maghrib* prayer for Princess Abtah, the ladies and servants. His hidden identity complies with the rules that a man must not be alone in a room with a woman who is not a blood relative. It is a moral offence. Women in Saudi Arabia must be disciplined enough to pray alone, in their homes. They are not allowed to go to the mosque for communal spiritual sustenance. I am privileged to witness this creatively devout gathering, a collective show of worship and love.

The oranges are ripe and give vibrant colour to the trees. I reach up to pick a small tangerine acutely aware of its sensuous fragrance and I savour each fresh succulent segment. There are many varieties of oranges in the Palace gardens.

"Bitter oranges make good marmalade," I explain to *Amira*, as we are on one of our garden walks.

"You – make marmalade?" she enquires. "Yes, every year, with Seville oranges from Spain." I reply.

"Good – we make on farm – marmalade nice English jam."

"No, not jam, Princess Abtah," I correct her. "Marmalade is made only from oranges; jam is made from all kinds of varieties of fruit, but not oranges." We walk on in silence. Sometimes I forget that she doesn't always catch what I say, and she is perhaps too proud to ask me to explain in a simpler way.

We make our third circular tour of the garden. By the fourth time round, tedium usually sets in for me. I go off into a daydream, in which I visualise myself sweating over a boiling cauldron of marmalade in the hot and airless farm kitchen.

Zahara, *Amira's* personal servant, ambles towards me. The pace of life is slow, no one hurries. The young women of Eritrea have facial bone structure, eyes, teeth and skin texture to be envied. Zahara's hair is bound up in a lilac coloured African turban. She wears a long, bright yellow, cheesecloth skirt, and a loose blouse of the same material over her motherly hips and bosom.

"Phee-lees," she calls to me in a leisurely voice: "Princess – say – c-u-u-mm!" I am filling my pockets with oranges. Fruit from the garden is free to all, but in a few days only the highest branches, out of my reach will be left unpicked.

I walk through the huge, bronze doors and up the long, sweeping staircase to the royal apartments. There is a lift which everybody uses except me. Occasionally Prince Muqrin and Princess Abtah use the stairs, presumably if they feel the need for exercise.

Princess Abtah's day sitting-room door is wide open, and bales of material cover the floor. Rose, the Palace seamstress is on her knees, scissors in hand, snipping off lengths of material under the watchful eye of the Princess. Muma Hasna, with a pensive expression, is holding up to her waist a length of dark blue material with large white spots.

"Take – Phyllis, you like – dress, or jacket and skirt?" *Amira* offers me a length of material not at all to my liking.

"Why, what's happening?" I ask, probably with a blank look on my face.

Amira explains, "Every *Ramadan* I give all – present for *Eid* – give Rose – she make."

I missed out last year, arriving at the end of *Ramadan*. My eyes search for plain fabric. All the women love bold, colourful patterns, and I don't want to end up coming face to face with my twin, or even my quadruplets!

Unlike the dressmakers and hairdressers in Hail, Rose is not a notorious gossip, though her workroom is inevitably a meeting place for news and information. Women come and go between duties and I can always rely on getting answers to perplexing questions about Palace life in there with her.

Rose came to Saudi Arabia from the Philippines to pay for her son in college. She is always in demand by the Royal Family, and the servants and their children. Repairing, altering, shortening, lengthening, designing and making clothes, she ploughs patiently through her piles of work. She is small, slim, calm and softly spoken and never too busy to help someone by taking on another odd job – no trouble! Rose represents dependability as well as continuity.

In her room the easy-going atmosphere, the mirrored walls that reflect light and movement, the laughter, chatter, cups of tea, the steady rhythm of the sewing machine, the ironing and the snip of scissors, create for me a special place to go, in some important way homely and consoling. I like Rose.

Chapter Twenty-one
Ramadan

The royal jet touches down by the VIP terminal at Jeddah airport. The royal entourage has arrived for the *Ramadan* holiday. The Princesses close their personal copies of the *Qur'an* and put them in their shoulder bags, handy for extra study during the month of *Ramadan*.

After the Royal Family has been whisked away, there is the usual scramble for the cars. A driver I do not recognise calls to me from his car.

"Phyllis – come with Filipino ladies!" Rose and Lynda move over for me to get in.

"All stay Makkah," Lynda informs me. "We go to Jeddah house."

This is news to me...and takes time to sink in. I am always the last to know what is going on. I realise Christians are not allowed into Makkah, but I didn't know I am going to be left alone in the Jeddah house.

"How long?" I ask apprehensively.

"Ten days. *Eid* – we go Hail." Ten days...what *am* I going to do with myself for ten days?

Tens of thousands of pilgrims from all over the world fly in to meet in equality before Allah. King Abdul Aziz airport covers the largest acreage in the world, the Hajj Terminal takes ten Jumbo jets at a time and the Saudi Arabian Government allocates three hundred million dollars a year to the Ministry of Pilgrimage. In this decade, the Kingdom spent seventy billion SR on Makkah and Madinah, including expanding the two holy mosques. Madinah based King Fahd Holy *Qur'an* printers have produced one hundred and twenty million copies of the *Qur'an*.

Pilgrims are organised into groups with leaders. Fitting so many people into two mosques and housing them in tents in the narrow Arafat valley is not easy. Pilgrims get segregated, lost or overcome with heat. My favourite Islamic author, Ruqaiyyah Waris Maqsud says, *'despite every obstacle there is a wonderful feeling of being one of a great family. Inconveniences and difficulties are brushed aside by the emotion, joy and triumph of being a pilgrim.'*

On Arafat plain the pilgrims erect a vast camp for two million. Mount Arafat is the mount of mercy where God reunited Adam and Eve. Standing before God in meditation and prayer, in the blistering heat, is the most important part of *Hajj*. A stony climb leads to the top and there a sermon is delivered to the people. Muslims believe this experience to have great mystical and emotional power, to be there with a repentant heart wipes out all past sins: life may begin anew.

In those four weeks, Muslims abstain from food, drink and sexual relations from first light until sundown. The sick, elderly, travellers and pregnant or nursing women may break the fast and make up an equal number of days later in the year. Children fast from puberty, or younger.

I saw an excited Sarah last year, in the arms of her admiring mother, full of praise that her daughter had fasted that day. A feeling of joy and achievement comes from each day's successful discipline and self-purification.

The aims of *swam*, the fast, are *'to develop self-control and overcome selfishness, greed and laziness; to restrain passion and appetite; to prepare for any real suffering that may be faced later; to experience hunger and thus develop sympathy for the poor; to gain spiritual strength and to experience companionship through shared ordeals.'*

Food to break the fast after sunset is *iftar*, consisting of a substantial soup, *shurba* with *sambusik*, triangular wafers filled with spicy meat and onion. More and bigger meals follow, with friends and relatives. An extra meal, *suhur*, can be squeezed in before first light. I am immersed in Muslim culture so this *Ramadan* makes me feel more of an outsider. I prepare my own meals during the day and join the servants or if I am invited, the family, for *iftar*.

The Jeddah house is the smallest family residence next door to Princess Hannah's house. The only place to walk is along a narrow path with a few trees and shrubs between the houses and the fortress walls. I feel hemmed in and despondent about my solitude, but also curiously challenged. Jeddah, the tourist guides write, is the city to visit in Saudi Arabia: *'You can't help but be caught up by the excitement of Jeddah. Perhaps nowhere else in the world do so many nationalities rub shoulders in such a strangely familiar way',* says the Berlitz Pocket guide.

Excitement? Well, this could be my opportunity.

I pull aside the heavy net curtains over the windows of my dreary claustrophobic and sparsely furnished bed-sit and peer out. A red Lamborghini is parked in the courtyard; I know it belongs to Prince Faisal, Princess Hannah's husband. Faisal clearly loves speed. Jo-Jo told me that, like his grandfather King Abdul Aziz, the prince is a skilled horseman and when they all lived in Hail he kept a fine Arab grey on the farm.

Arab horses are descendants of the wild *kuhaylan* and ancestors of the thoroughbred, noted for their intelligence, beauty, speed and stamina. Grey is what horsey people call a white horse, and an Arabian horseman galloping across the hot golden desert on a white horse is a romantic picture, especially as Prince Faisal is very handsome. He is around thirty, and I have heard gossip about the house he owns in the mountains in Ta'if, 1700 feet above sea level, a cool refuge from the summer heat and where the roses for my favourite scent are grown.

Moving away from the window, I fill the kettle and set it to boil. A pot of tea will put me in a better frame of mind. Tea and milk have been left for me by Princess Hannah's housekeeper. Sipping the welcome brew I thumb through my diary: Jeddah… Jeddah…Ah yes…the British Consulate! My sudden outburst and jump to my feet sends a cockroach scurrying for cover.

No telephone in my room, I hurry out and eventually find one in the hallway. I dial the number.

"Oh, well, you see… I'm in Jeddah for the *Ramadan* holiday and…well I would like to meet some other expats…"

"Come along tonight, we are having an open evening, £8.50, from 8.00pm to 11.00pm. Free food, buy your own drinks."

I put the phone down. Fantastic!

My elation soon subsides. Who will drive me there? I remember a warning about immigrant taxi drivers sexually harassing women travelling on their own – it's a risk.

'Get a yellow cab with a black stripe; some of the drivers speak English,' I am told. There is no telephone contact number or central office for them and I don't have the number for the expensive white limousine service. Managing to squeeze into one of my favourite dresses which shows quite a lot of leg, I go over my plan to get to the Consulate. I will ask Princess Hannah's workman Orlando to escort me down to the main road, and then…

I dismiss several taxis, I just don't like the look of the drivers. I begin to feel edgy…and ridiculously conspicuous. Orlando hails a yellow cab, a Filipino pulls up.

"Can you take me to the British Consulate please?" I search his face for tell-tale clues to unacceptable behaviour. He frowns, and thinks for a few seconds. Orlando mumbles to him in their own language. "Yes, Ma'am," he replies.

"How much?" I ask.

"Thirty six SR" comes the reply.

"Good price, Ma'am - he OK." Orlando says approvingly, giving the thumbs-up sign, a broad grin on his youthful face.

Arriving safely outside the Consulate I ask my driver to come back for me at 11.00pm. I check in with my passport at the security gate and make my way through a neat garden, past an inviting looking swimming pool to a sign: 'This way to British Club.' The hubbub of a language I know so well, the 'jolly' atmosphere so associated with the English, draws me magnetically into a packed room. I am there. It seems like a dream.

Chapter Twenty-two
In Expat Society

Waiting to be served, at a packed bar with three bartenders working their socks off – the experience feels surreal. Here I am with one sole objective in mind: a gin and tonic! On this patch of British territory, I have a craving I have disciplined myself not to think about while I am in Saudi Arabia. Bizarre. Onto my second gin and tonic, getting used to talking to men and women in my own wonderful language I sit with a group of British teachers who work at a private British school. They live in a compound, a complex of houses and flats exclusively for westerners.

"If you want a game of tennis, or a swim in the compound pool, give me a ring…Why don't you come along with us to the expat beach…? Let's make a date…" I have a great time and I don't stop talking. Telephone numbers are exchanged and Sue, a bubbly blond music teacher gives me a copy of the Jeddah News, a monthly pamphlet of news and events in privately run clubs for Jeddah's expat community, a lifeline for people like me.

Around eleven we all walk back to the security gate together, we girls dressed once again in our *abayas*.

"The Saudi police patrol outside," warns Sue's husband Mark. "A couple of guys were arrested a few months ago for taking away cans of beer. Can we drop you off at your home?" I look anxiously for my driver. Ah, there he is, waiting patiently.

"No thanks. Good night." Everyone hurries, keen to get away from prying eyes and the still, humid night air, into their cars.

The events of the evening inspire me to muse on the promised excitement of Jeddah.

Breathe the sea air
A fresh wind blows through Jeddah!
Cosmopolitan, international - open society?
"Don't remove your abaya, Ma'am
You could be fooled"
"But I saw a girl in shorts!"
"Well, she was a westerner and in the compound.
The security man is at the gate."

The compound bus is leaving for the ladies shopping trip...
Forbidden by law to drive,
Woman's dependency for mobility
Increases male supremacy.

Lucy, trim in her multicoloured bikini,
sits by the compound pool reading...
Splash! A glistening spray soaks her page...
Ha - a - ah! Italian men are so...
"Buon giorno, Lucy." Two more surround her lounger
She gazes into dark, liquid eyes - and smiles
Remembering their home-made wine.

The lift sails up to the roof-top restaurant
Fresh fish for lunch in the Intercontinental Hotel...heavenly
Oh! and MEN, in suits and ties...
A cacophony of languages fills the air
Drifting out over the Red Sea.

It's amazing what alcohol can do for the imagination. I feel happy to be slightly in control of my life. I will make the most of the opportunity. A trip to the supermarket, to stock up the fridge in my bed-sit is a necessity. Princess Hannah's cook is on hand for a late evening meal tonight.

"Please come here" I point to the house as the driver pulls up outside, "tomorrow morning, nine o'clock." I held up nine fingers, "We go Abhur." Abhur is the name of the expat beach.

"Beach, OK?" He nods. "OK, Ma'am." I pay him and agree on a price to the beach.

Handing over 30SR to be by the sea for a day is reasonable. Changing facilities are clean with toilets and showers. I leave my *abaya* and clothes in a locker, feeling odd walking around practically naked.

In the glorious setting I feel self-conscious on my own, especially as my bikini is meant for a slimmer figure, and find a cane chair set by a table in a secluded spot under a leafy palm tree. The temperature this late December must be about eighty degrees Fahrenheit and a limpid turquoise sea lies at the edge of the private white sand beach. Smothering myself with sun cream and protecting my body with a very large sun hat and sunglasses, I settle down to read.

"Hi, Phyllis – you made it then?" Sue and her husband Mark stand over me togged up for snorkelling. "Here," Mark hands me equipment. "This coral reef has the best marine life in the world – it's like the Great Barrier Reef in Oz. Come and see for yourself." Soaking up the relaxing atmosphere, I have just reached the denouement of the novel I am reading, and don't want to move.

"I don't know anything about snorkelling." Reluctantly, I walk to the end of the wooden pier out into the sea. Sue warns me about stone fish, which eject a deadly poison.

"Put your sneakers on. Thank God they've got rubber soles!" Going down steps into shallow water, Mark alerts me that the shallow coral table drops abruptly to a great depth several hundred metres out. The reef acts as a barrier to sharks. Well, a bit of excitement is what I was looking for.

This, the very first snorkelling expedition I have ever been on, is a revelation. I am so glad I have come. The water is crystal clear, accentuating pink and purple coral. Brilliantly coloured fish of all shapes, sizes and markings dart and glide, another world floating before my eyes. Not feeling very confident, I keep in easy reach of Sue and Mark. He *has* mentioned sharks.

Safely back on the beach, we sip exotic fruit cocktails through straws, sun ourselves and soak up the blissful surroundings. I pinch myself: no, I am not dreaming.

"Darling, lovely to hear from you!" For a couple of days I have been trying to contact Faiza. I know she is also in Jeddah for the *Ramadan* holiday. She is always hard to reach.

"I'm in Princess Abtah's house here in Jeddah, everyone is in Makkah, can we meet?"

"Darling, all alone? That's terrible! I'll take you out to dinner – do you like Chinese food?" I like any meal I can get. My domestic arrangements are very unpredictable.

"Yes, yes…of course, when, and what time?"

"What about tomorrow night? You know at *Ramadan* everyone eats late? Say about ten?"

"Thanks so much Faiza, I'm looking forward to seeing you." I put the phone down.

It is 1.00pm on my third day in Jeddah. What can I do for the rest of the day? I wander outside into the courtyard, past Princess Hannah's servants' quarters, the kitchen, the bedrooms then, glancing through the vast expanse of glass to a reception room, I see Princess Hannah painting a canvas. I stop, hoping she will see me, but she looks engrossed in her work. I move nearer to the window, I am intrigued to see what she is painting. Glancing up, she notices me and goes over to the security buzzer to let me in.

"This – picture – English sea – very big waves – windy. Clouds – change – move quickly." Princess Hannah had taken a photograph of a rough sea when she visited Margate in Kent for the day. The effect she has created from the snapshot and her memory expresses a typical English grey summer sea-scape, which I know Princess Abtah and Princess Hannah love. She has just returned from Madinah.

"Pray in mosque of Prophet – good – all people – same before Allah," she says with conviction and adds that for once women can uncover their faces, because no man should look at them with lust at the time of pilgrimage. All normal clothing is put away, women wear plain, undecorated, long-sleeved, ankle-length shifts with bare hands and feet.

'These clothes symbolise three things: equality, single-mindedness and self-sacrifice' says Ruqaiyyah in *Islam*.

"Wait, Phyllis – I have – for you" she goes away to her bedroom, returning with a small black velvet box in her hand. "This – present from Madinah – for you." Inside is a silver pendant, a single rose carved onto the ornate oval framed setting. I thank her for thinking of me. "You – like go – Makkah?"

"I'd love to", prohibition always provokes my curiosity.

Before I leave Princess Hannah rings Orlando to take me to her seaside house. Orlando skippered Prince Faisal's motor cruiser. In English essays Bander writes about deep sea diving expeditions from the cruiser; how the first dive with his instructor is the most fantastic experience of his young life, and about Sharam Abhur, a seaside playground for water sports. Beaches do not cater for tourists. Visitors who come to Jeddah are pilgrims. Sunning myself by the swimming pool on the patio of Princess Hannah's house, I watch Orlando's snorkel air pipe drift further and further away.

I look at my watch: 11.00pm. Where is Faiza? I ring her number:

no reply. 'All dressed up and nowhere to go,' I say to myself, putting on my *abaya* and walking out towards the security gate. The Turkish caretaker Nica, who mans the gate, salutes me:

"Where you go?"

"I don't know…a friend…she's coming." I always leave a message for Princess Hannah, letting her know who I am with. A car horn hoots. Nodding his head Nica opens the huge sliding security doors.

"Sorry, darling," Faiza has a car full of children with her, "we take the little ones to my mother and their nanny, then we go, OK?" She has just picked them up from a children's party given in an adventure playground rented for the occasion. "Shops stay open until two-thirty at *Ramadan*, you know Phyllis….Before we eat I must buy dress material, my dressmaker is coming tomorrow, and …oh yes darling, I must get some tablets from my doctor, my hair is falling out!"

Faiza's driver parks the car on the Corniche, ten minutes walk away from the Sheraton Hotel. By the time we reach the front entrance of the hotel we are heckled and waved at from passing cars. I am irritated, Faiza just says in patronising and dismissive tones: "They love to flirt, darling. We'll have a drink here, before we go on to the Chinese Restaurant."

Through the tropical garden entrance, lit by tiny coloured lights, I follow her down steps to a small lake covered with water lilies. Here I stop, amazed at what I see: on one side of the lake women sit at tables, the uniform black of their *abayas* hinting, as always, at a mysterious conspiracy, while all the men sit at tables on the other side of the lake in robes and *ghutrahs*. Faiza sweeps through, with a wave of her hand.

"They eat here…we go to the café. Come, Phyllis."

"Do they ever speak to each other?" I can't get over the scene.

"Oh no, darling," Faiza leans closer, and whispers, "but they leave their phone number on the table of someone they like, as they are passing by!"

Faiza is a generous woman. She orders fresh fish and lobster dishes, with the dishes of the day the restaurant manager has recommended. She talks about her visit to Makkah in a reverent way, with a string of superlatives, as do all the Muslim women who love telling me about Makkah. Faiza and I have ideas about improving Saudi female education, her hobby-horse. She wants to visit London with her eldest daughter next summer, but she hints at difficulties, she will have to persuade her husband.

"He's not like Prince Muqrin."

I suggest we meet for coffee one morning, at the Sheraton, before we return to Hail.

"Darling!" she is shocked, "don't you know? During *Ramadan* all bars, cafés and restaurants are closed all day. The city's dead; everyone who doesn't go to work is asleep until midday or later. Fasting for us means we can't even take a sip of water. And even non-Muslims risk deportation if they eat, drink or smoke in public during the day."

"What about cheating?" I can't resist the question.

"You can never deceive Allah," Faiza replies piously.

We go on to a chic open-air café near the sea, for coffee. A woman sitting near us is smoking a hubble-bubble pipe.

"What is she smoking?"

"A light mixture of tobacco and dried fruit" Faiza looks disapproving, "I hate the smell of smoke, let's move." Settling down at a table amongst shrubs and trees, I revel in the enormous soft enveloping pale pink velvet sofa, the pink and white mosaic floor - palm trees, flying dolphin and fish fountains: a sensuous atmosphere, in the balmy night sea air. We sit there for a good time, enjoying each other's company, and our freedom, not wanting to move.

Back in the heavy traffic along the Corniche, I am wide awake with the buzz and night life of the city. Faiza has style. I am sorry to leave her when we part at 3.00am. Day is night and night is day during *Ramadan*.

Time passes too quickly. So much for my fears about loneliness and boredom. Sue and Mark take me out in their boat, and we moor in a lagoon for the day, to fish, picnic and snorkel further, and my confidence grows slowly but surely. My long desire to ride a camel is fulfilled. Sadly it is not in a romantic desert setting, with the heat shimmering like that wonderful shot in the Lawrence of Arabia film but in the gardens along the Corniche. Touristy if you like, but not to be missed!

Fortified by the memory of my brief social whirl, I am happy to sit and chat to Lynda and Rose and the servants in Princess Hannah's house. Bernice has a favourite story she loves to tell about a governess who complained of extreme boredom and locked herself for two days in her room not answering any calls or knocking on her door.

When she eventually emerged she was invited to join the Royal Family for *iftar*, an honour as the meal after fasting is a sacred family gathering, and during the feast she recited 'The Mad Hatter's Tea Party' from *Alice In Wonderland*, a story which obsessed her.

"They – say – lady – mad," says Linda. This was the governess who walked around the Palace gardens reading *Alice* aloud at the top of her voice. I can empathise with the woman's feelings. We all show our pent-up emotions in different ways and there are days when I think I too could easily go a little crazy out here.

Chapter Twenty-three
The Silken Bonds

The *Eid-al-fitre* holiday has ended and January brings unsettling days for me. My eldest son, Richard, is to marry in April. I feel I want to be there for him. I badly wish to go home. And Saddam Hussain's face glowers threateningly on my TV screen; conflict in Iraq has reared its ugly head. I am restless – maybe the break in Jeddah has spoiled me. Jo-Jo and Bander's new timetable has so little time for English study with me. Warning bells are ringing.

I turn round slowly, looking at my reflection in the panels of mirrors around my room. I have changed. The discoveries and the self-discovery of the past year, the enormous effort I have made to adapt to, and integrate with, Saudi society, absorbing the whole experience, have filled me to bursting. I stand still for some time, looking, listening, waiting for an instinctive guiding hand. I can feel the rhythms of life moving me on.

Once again, I am faced with how to resolve my problem without conflict, to allow everyone concerned to extricate themselves without losing face. My brain whirls. If only I had someone to talk to, to discuss my problems with and to help me. I can't tell anyone at all. Not here. It will give great offence. Not at home, for fear my plan would backfire and cause disappointment.

The last words a friend said to me at home were, "How will you escape?" It was a highly perceptive question. I do feel I am a prisoner in this most luxurious of prisons. I am, I suppose, tied by bonds of affection and respect, for the Royal Family and for the traditions of loyalty and long service which are in Arab culture, and are impossible for me – or anyone of sensibility – to set aside lightly.

So yes, I am secretly planning my escape. After careful thought I decide to arrange for my departure slowly, step by step. I have achieved a long ambition to experience the Middle East, and have saved money, another prime objective. My role as an English governess has never been clearly defined and is rather left up to me. Sometimes the very fact that I am English and symbolically here, seem to be all that is really required.

I do remember Princess Abtah setting out her objectives for Bander's studies when I first arrived. She wanted Bander to master English vocabulary and grammar for:

1. How to open a bank account in an English bank.
2. How to book accommodation at a hotel.
3. How to reserve a table at a restaurant by telephone.
4. How to book a holiday at a tourist office.
5. How to prepare a Curriculum Vitae.
6. How to understand the menu, order a meal and pay the bill.

She asked me to give her lessons on the last topic, especially for Italian restaurants which are her favourite. I taught her the language for shopping for clothes, jewellery and perfume, and for buying, preparing and cooking French, Italian, English and American dishes.

The advantages of a day off, to get away, a refreshing change are denied me. Where can I go, and how? I've won more freedom for myself than other governesses had, who I think never ventured beyond the Palace walls on their own.

My experience has been an ordeal in many ways but some risk in our lives does enable us to find out what we are capable of. We all strive to survive each day, and to survive in an alien place does need extra effort. Travel will make one stronger, more resilient, and more open to relish differences in life-styles and cultures.

The pattern of Palace life continues into another year, familiar now but never predictable. I get delightful surprises on occasions: to see Jo-Jo and Bander sitting together opposite me in the study room, attentive and more or less punctual; and one day, Sarah saying, out of the blue – in the high-handed way she loves to adopt:

"Ba-Ba (Pa-Pa) pleased with Phyllis. I hate study English – but with you – OK."

None of which makes what I am planning to do any easier.

At the beginning of February, I know I have to make my first move. I will read my son Richard's letter to Princess Abtah. Lamia is with her in the day sitting-room. They are busy planning catering and accommodation for a residential business meeting Prince Muqrin will host on his farm. The timing is wrong, I have chosen a bad moment.

"Oh, I'm sorry, I'll come back later," I say, not wishing to intrude. It is typical of Princess Abtah that she is not irritated or annoyed at my presence, but welcomes me into the room:

"Sit, Phyllis – what you say?" I feel embarrassed.

"Er…er…well, my son is getting married," I read from the letter, "and…well you see, I must go back to England."

Amira checks a list in front of her and, not looking up, she asks, "When – you go – how long?"

"March." I want time before the wedding to help prepare for it. I avoid saying for how long.

"OK," she responds. I can see she is preoccupied, which is to my advantage. I slip out quietly. This is the first step…at least she knows I will be going in March, and the rest will have to unfold as time will have it.

The news from Iraq is grim, I don't care to be living so close to the border. Plans are underway for American war planes to be stationed in Kuwait.

My internal telephone rings: "May I speak to Phyllis Ellis?" a cultured English voice enquires.

"Yes, hello, I'm Phyllis." I wonder who on earth it can be.

"This is James Howard, I'm ringing from the British Embassy in Riyadh." I gulp. The thought races through my mind that he is ringing to warn expats about the conflict in Iraq.

"We received your name and details from our Consulate in Jeddah – we had no idea we had an expat living in such a remote area. I'm calling to check you have access to a phone for international calls, and are happy about your situation and your avenues of communication to us if need be."

"Yes, I'm fine, I've been here a year now. Thanks for your call, I suppose I should have contacted you earlier." We carry on chatting – I need to hear his voice, and feel strangely reassured when he gives me his office and home phone numbers. His call is the support I was looking for.

The office ring to let me know my flight has been booked for March 6th. My next problem is excess baggage. It has been a busy week for Ahmed, transporting guests from Hail airport for Prince Muqrin and running errands to and from the farm. I manage to persuade him to take my heaviest luggage to the airport cargo office.

"You come back – Palace after wedding?" Ahmed likes to know what is going on.

"*Insh'Allah!*" I reply.

I am ticking off the days. Gabby arrives to help Princess Abtah with the arrangements for the farm. The best way to let *Amira* know something you find difficult to tell her is to spill the beans to Gabby:

"My family are worried about my safety here, with the conflict in Iraq. They don't want me to return to Saudi Arabia after the wedding."

"Honey, I was here in the war, nothing's gonna happen to you darlin' – you stick around, the kids need their English."

Well, I have said it; soon it will reach *Amira's* ears and spread round the grape-vine. That very evening as we all sit as we do most nights, drinking coffee and mint tea in the *diwaniyah*, Princess Abtah leans across her chair and speaks to me, her face passive and unsmiling.

"You – not happy in Palace, Phyllis? You not come back after wedding?"

"I'm not unhappy, Princess Abtah, my family are worried about me," I reply. She doesn't pursue the conversation, her face shows no response and she says nothing. I am leaving of my own volition, the ambiguity of my situation suits me, I feel as if I've kept my options a little bit open. I might easily have a change of heart. Soha echoes my ambivalent feelings.

"You go home – spend all money. Say – no good here – I go back – Palace."

My bags are packed. I've given my toaster, teapot, iron, ironing board and pot plants to Hanna, Rahma and Nefisa. Life is going on around me as before, I am slipping quietly away…it is almost an anticlimax to all that has gone before. I have no regrets and am glad that I took the risk. The experience has affected me in a profound and positive way, I have had a social, cultural and religious re-education.

I have learned so much about a country that is rich not only materially, but with the spiritual riches of Islam, and seen the infinite and awe-inspiring desert, and the changes oil wealth has brought. A massive investment in irrigation has brought life, green fields and orchards to the desert and self-sufficiency in wheat, poultry, eggs and dairy products. There is still so much to do, especially for women, in education and health, but progress is greater than could ever have been apparent to me from Essex.

"No more English!" Sarah beams, giving me a bead bracelet she has made for me as a parting gift. Jo-Jo hugs me, a wistful look on her face. "I'll miss you, Phyllis."

"I'll miss you too," I reply, tears suddenly burning the back of my eyes. We shared together, and with Bander, a special relationship, unique, never to be forgotten.

"I've come to say goodbye." Princess Abtah and I embrace for the first time, but as we move away from each other, I can see by her face she is uneasy.

"What time – you fly?"

"One hour," I reply. I don't want to linger, my emotions might get the better of me. "I'll miss you all..." I say moving away.

"Thank you Phyllis" is all she says.

I hurry down the sweeping staircase, out of the huge bronze door and into the waiting car. The flight prayer heralds my departure. I check my air ticket – it is a return. But as the plane takes off, I know I won't be coming back.

"It's cellulite!" I lie naked on my aroma therapist's treatment couch. "However did you get yourself in this state, you're out of shape, especially your legs, stomach and bottom, where has your girlish figure gone, gal?" Sally was a nursing sister before she qualified as an aroma therapist and reflexologist, and she stands no nonsense, giving the bad news straight from the shoulder. She is a good neighbour and friend.

"Well, I tried to keep to a sensible diet. I swam every day and exercised."

"These foreign countries, you never know how they are going to affect you, do you? If you ask me you came back not a minute too soon," she lectures.

As the aroma of the essential oils and the skilled massage do their work, I think about the past few days since I arrived home. Feeling exhausted, I sleep for long hours, as if I have returned from an expedition to some distant mountain peak. The change in temperature doesn't help. I dig out woolly vests and stockings, and make porridge for breakfast. But there is nothing so blissful as coming home. However much I travel, I need to know I have family, love and roots to return to, a privilege I cherish.

My family are coming to lunch. I wait in my *abaya*, *tarha* and *burqa*, curious to see their reaction. At the first sight of me, as I open the front door, my daughter-in-law to be, Alison, lets out a shocked scream, her face screws up in disgust.

"Ugh, horrible, how could you walk about like that?"

"Take it off Mum, you're giving us the creeps," my younger son Jason says, "the sight of you dressed like that …"

Well, it is a bit unfair of me. Maybe seeing me in Saudi Arabia, in the true environment, they would find me more acceptable!

To prepare a meal for my family gives me great joy, especially as I am able to buy nutritious, unfattening ingredients. I am so eager to give them presents. For my son Jason, a handsome camel cloak, a *bisht*, edged with beautifully woven gold braid. Prince Abdul Aziz, Lamia's husband gave it to me especially for Jason, when I was staying with them in their luxurious Riyadh house and I was downhearted because I couldn't get to Jordan.

Wall plaques, designed with *Qur'anic* verse or script, are fashionable gifts in Saudi Arabia as are prayer beads. My family accept these with the hugs and kisses I'd missed so much.

I catch up with all their news. The yacht racing adventures of my elder son Richard, who tells me he won the 'John Franks Trophy' which we donated to the Island Sailing Club at Cowes in memory of his father … a poignant and wonderful achievement, strangely on the very date of his father's death two years ago.

Then there are Jason's flying stories with the Royal Marines.

I don't like to hear about the time the engine of his Gazelle failed - there's no baling out of helicopters - but he and his co-pilot successfully landed the aircraft. A Green Endorsement from Naval Aviation, plus my son safe and well by my side, add up to a very proud moment for me.

I can give Richard my mother's antique gold wedding ring for Alison, and think of spending some Saudi savings on a stylish wedding outfit. Jason is to be best man and says marriage is not on his own agenda yet. I have missed the intimacy of family conversation when I can be myself, off guard, relaxed, like nowhere else.

Already I can feel myself settling with relish into the new life that is beginning, but I will always be grateful to my Saudi Royal Family for the privilege of the adventure, for the experience of reviving and upholding the honourable Victorian tradition of the English governess abroad, but above all for giving me the time and space to become my own woman.

Saudi Lady
The burden of Eve is upon you.
Swathe thyself in black from head to toe,
And mourn...mourn for your gender.

Show him not thy face,
Lest his desires seduce you.
Glance not his way,
It is a sin.

Men's eyes undress,
Men's eyes caress,
Men's eyes...

She fears to walk alone,
Kerb crawling males,
Cassette players blaring,
Accost and flirt,
Laughing loudly.
Car hooters blast her way.
Female alone? She could be escaping!
Hound her in!
The huge door slams.

Men's eyes undress,
Men's eyes caress,
Men's eyes...

Cover me, I am a temptress,
My body sensuous and alluring.
It is not my own but a male prerogative,
I dreamed of the evolution of Eve...
Black robes were shed,
I stood alone,
My own woman.

Other Titles from TravellersEye

Discovery Road

Authors: Tim Garratt & Andy Brown
Editor: Dan Hiscocks

ISBN: 0953057534
R.R.P: £7.99

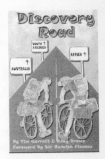

Their mission and dream was to cycle around the southern hemisphere of the planet, with just two conditions. Firstly the journey must be completed within 12 months, and secondly, the cycling duo would have no support team or backup vehicle, just their determination, friendship and pedal power.

"Readers will surely find themselves reassessing their lives and be inspired to reach out and follow their own dreams."

Sir Ranulph Fiennes, Explorer

Fever Trees of Borneo

Author: Mark Eveleigh
Editor: Gordon Medcalf

ISBN: 095357569
R.R.P: £7.99

This is the story of how two Englishmen crossed the remotest heights of central Borneo, using trails no western eye had seen before, in search of the legendary 'Wild Men of Borneo'. On the way they encounter shipwreck, malaria, amoebic dysentery, near starvation, leeches, exhaustion, enforced alcohol abuse and barbecued mouse-deer foetus.

"Mark has the kind of itchy feet which will take more than a bucket of Johnson's baby talc to cure... he has not only stared death in the face, he has poked him in the ribs and insulted his mother."

(Observer)

Frigid Women

Authors: Sue & Victoria Riches
Editor: Gordon Medcalf

ISBN: 0953057526
R.R.P: £7.99

In 1997 a group of twenty women set out to become the world's first all female expedition to the North Pole. Mother and daughter, Sue and Victoria Riches were amongst them. Follow the expedition's adventures in this true life epic of their struggle to reach one of Earth's most inhospitable places, suffering both physical and mental hardships in order to reach their goal, to make their dream come true.

"This story is a fantastic celebration of adventure, friendship, courage and love. Enjoy it all you would be adventurers and dream on."

Dawn French

Riding with Ghosts

Author: Gwen Maka
Editor: Gordon Medcalf

ISBN: 1903070007
R.R.P: £7.99

This is the frank, often outrageous account of a forty-something Englishwoman's epic 4,000 mile cycle ride from Seattle to Mexico, via the snow covered Rocky Mountains. She travels the length and breadth of the American West, mostly alone and camping in the wild. She runs appalling risks and copes in a gutsy, hilarious way with exhaustion, climatic extremes, dangerous animals, eccentrics, lechers and a permanently saddle-sore bum.

We share too her deep involvement with the West's pioneering past, and with the strong, often tragic traces history has left lingering on the land.

A Trail of Visions

Guide books tell you where to go, what to do and how to do it. A Trail of Visions shows and tells you how it feels.

"A Trail of Visions tells with clarity what it is like to follow a trail, both the places you see and the people you meet."

Independent on Sunday

"The illustrated guide."

The Times

Route 1: India, Sri Lanka, Thailand, Sumatra

Photographer / Author: Vicki Couchman

Editor:Dan Hiscocks

ISBN: 1871349338

R.R.P: £14.99

Route 2: Peru, Bolivia, Ecuador, Columbia

Photographer / Author: Vicki Couchman

Editor:Dan Hiscocks

ISBN: 093505750X

R.R.P: £16.99

Slow Winter
Author: Alex Hickman

ISBN: 0953057585

R.R.P: £7.99

Haunted by his late father's thirst for adventure Alex persuaded his local paper that it needed a Balkan correspondent. Talking his way into besieged Sarajevo, he watched as the city's fragile cease fire fell apart. A series of chance encounters took him to Albania and a bizarre appointment to the government. Thrown into an alliance with the country's colourful dissident leader, he found himself occupying a ringside seat as corruption and scandal spilled the country into chaos.

This is a moving story of one man's search for his father's legacy among the mountains and ruin of Europe's oldest, and most mysterious corner.

Tea for Two…with no cups
Author: Polly Benge
Editor: Dan Hiscocks

ISBN: 0953057593

R.R.P: £7.99

Four months before her 30th birthday Polly finds herself in a quandary. Fed up with dancing a swan or woodland nymph every night, failing to impress Barry Manilow with her singing abilities and falling in love with a New Zealander with a rapidly expiring visa she needs to come up with some answers quickly. She decides the only way to do this is by embarking on a 'love test'. With a yet uncalloused bottom she joins Tim and Lee on a bicycle ride from Kathmandu to Assam in the hope of finding some answers.

The Jungle Beat – fighting terrorists in Malaya

Author: Roy Follows
Editor: Dan Hiscocks

ISBN: 0953057577
R.R.P: £7.99

This book describes, in his own words, the experiences of a British officer in the Malayan Police during the extended Emergency of the 1950's. It is the story of a ruthless battle for survival against an environment and an enemy which were equally deadly. It ranks with the toughest and grimmest of the latter-day SAS adventures.

" It tells the story with no holds barred: war as war is. A compelling reminder of deep jungle operations."

General Sir Peter de la Billière

Touching Tibet

Author: Niema Ash
Editor: Dan Hiscocks

ISBN: 0953057550
R.R.P: £7.99

After the Chinese invasion of 1950, Tibet remained closed to travellers until 1984. When the borders were briefly re-opened, Niema Ash was one of the few people fortunate enough to visit the country before the Chinese re-imposed their restrictions in 1987. *Touching Tibet* is a vivid, compassionate, poignant but often amusing account of a little known ancient civilisation and a unique and threatened culture.

"Excellent - Niema Ash really understands the situation facing Tibet and conveys it with remarkable perception."

Tenzin Choegyal (brother of The Dalai Lama)

Heaven & Hell

An eclectic collection of anecdotal travel stories – the best from thou of competition entries.

"...an inspirational experience. I couldn't wait to leave the count encounter the next inevitable disaster." The Independer

Travellers' Tales from Heaven & Hell

Author: Various
Editor: Dan Hiscocks

ISBN: 0953057
R.R.P: £6.99

More Travellers' Tales from Heaven & Hell

Author: Various
Editor: Dan Hiscocks

ISBN: 1903
R.R.P: £6.9

TravellersEye Club Membership

Each month we receive hundreds of enquiries from people who've read our books or entered our competitions. All of these people have one thing in common: an aching to achieve something extraordinary, outside the bounds of our everyday lives. Not everyone can undertake the more extreme challenges, but we all value learning about other people's experiences.

Membership is free because we want to unite people of similar interests. Via our website, members will be able to liase with each other about everything from the kit they've taken, to the places they've been to and the things they've done. Our authors will also be available to answer any of your questions if you're planning a trip or if you simply have a question about their books.

As well as regularly up-dating members with news about our forthcoming titles, we will also offer you the following benefits:

Free entry to author talks / signings
Direct author correspondence
Discounts off new and past titles
Free entry to TravellersEye events
Discounts on a variety of travel products and services

To register your membership, simply write or email us telling us your name and address (postal and email). See address at the front of this book.